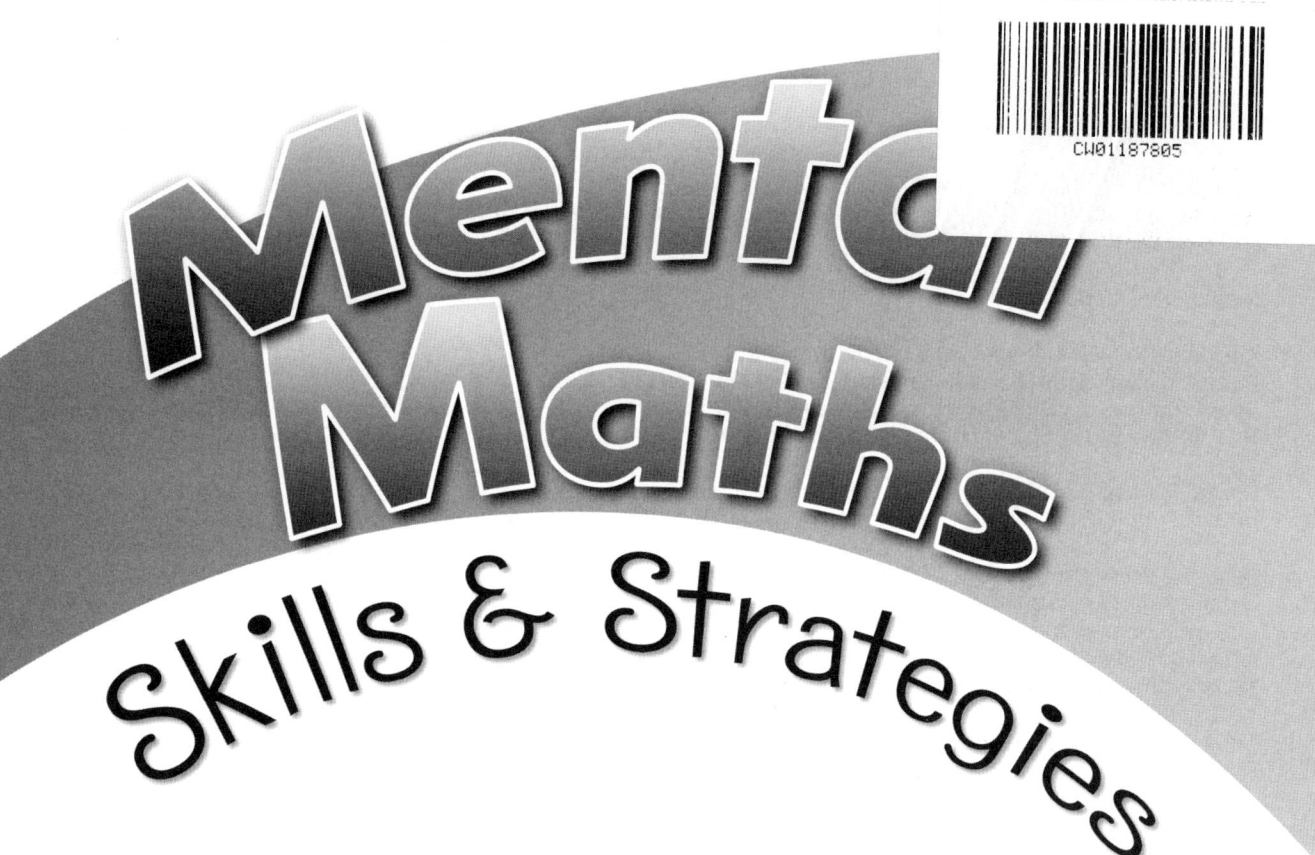

Mental Maths
Skills & Strategies

Book 5

Andrew J. Woods

OXFORD
UNIVERSITY PRESS

OXFORD
UNIVERSITY PRESS

Great Clarendon Street, Oxford OX2 6DP

Oxford University Press is a department of the University of Oxford.
It furthers the University's objective of excellence in research, scholarship,
and education by publishing worldwide in

Oxford New York

Auckland Bangkok Buenos Aires Cape Town Chennai
Dar es Salaam Delhi Hong Kong Istanbul Karachi Kolkata
Kuala Lumpur Madrid Melbourne Mexico City Mumbai
Nairobi São Paulo Shanghai Taipei Tokyo Toronto

Oxford is a registered trade mark of Oxford University Press
in the UK and in certain other countries

Original text written by Andrew J. Woods
© Andrew J. Woods 2002

Adapted text written by Lucy Simonds
© Oxford University Press 2004

The moral rights of the author have been asserted
Database right Oxford University Press (maker)

This edition first published 2004
Published by arrangement with Oxford University Press, Melbourne

All rights reserved. No part of this publication may be reproduced,
stored in a retrieval system, or transmitted, in any form or by any means,
without the prior permission in writing of Oxford University Press, or as
expressly permitted by law, or under terms agreed with the appropriate
reprographics rights organisation

Only those pages bearing the instruction
© OUP: Copying permitted for purchasing school only
may be photocopied accordingly

Enquiries concerning reproduction outside the scope of the above should
be sent to the Rights Department, Oxford University Press, at the address above

You must not circulate this book in any other binding or cover
and you must impose this same condition on any acquirer

British Library Cataloguing in Publication Data

Data available

ISBN 0 19 836097 5
10 9 8 7 6 5 4 3 2

Original design by Leigh Ashforth @ watershed art & design
Illustrated by Luke Jurevicius
Cover photograph by Alex Macnaughton
Typeset by Fakenham Photosetting Ltd, Norfolk
Printed in Great Britain by Ashford Colour Press, Gosport, Hants

Contents

Introduction 4	
Learning Objectives 5	
NNS Framework Matching Chart. 6	
Mathematics 5–14 Matching Chart 7	
Mental Skills and Strategies 8	

Unit	page
1 Number Facts 10
2 Extended Number Facts 11
3 Counting and Order. 12
4 Measurement: Length 13
5 Place Value 14
➡ REVIEW 1 15
Take a Break 1. 16
6 Number Facts 17
7 Money 18
8 Fractions 19
9 Decimals 20
10 Equations 21
➡ REVIEW 2 22
Take a Break 2. 23
11 Number Facts 24
12 Measurement: Time 25
13 Fractions and Decimals. 26
14 Place Value 27
15 Doubling and Halving 28
➡ REVIEW 3 29
Take a Break 3. 30
16 Number Facts 31
17 Equations 32
18 Measurement: Mass 33
19 Percentages 34
20 Counting and Order. 35
➡ REVIEW 4 36
Take a Break 4. 37

21 Number Facts 38
22 Extended Number Facts 39
23 Measurement: Capacity 40
24 Equations 41
25 Counting and Order. 42
➡ REVIEW 5 43
Take a Break 5. 44
26 Number Facts 45
27 Money 46
28 Factors 47
29 Fractions and Decimals 48
30 Place Value 49
➡ REVIEW 6 50
Take a Break 6. 51
31 Number Facts 52
32 Square Numbers 53
33 Measurement: Tine 54
34 Counting and Order. 55
35 Equations 56
➡ REVIEW 7 57
Take a Break 7. 58
36 Number Facts 59
37 Area and Perimeter 60
38 Fractions, Decimals, Percentages 61
39 Measurement 62
40 Terms 63
➡ REVIEW 8 64
Take a Break 8. 65
Important Facts. 66
Class Record Sheet 67
Pupil's Progress Chart 68
Listen and Write 70
Answers 74

Introduction

An ability to calculate mentally lies at the heart of numeracy.
(National Numeracy Strategy *Framework for Teaching Mathematics*)

The ability to make quick mental calculations is one that is essential in becoming confident with calculation. The exercises in this book are organised according to key skills and are designed to provide opportunities for children to practise skills that they will need to use regularly - both in class and in life. The *Mental Maths Skills and Strategies* series focuses on effective teaching of mental calculation strategies, thereby increasing confidence in all areas of numeracy.

This book contains 40 topic-related Units. Each Unit is referenced to one or more learning objectives to enable you to incorporate the activities into your planning. These learning objectives are summarised in the table on page 5 for ease of reference. The grids on pages 6 and 7 show how the Units can be matched to appropriate strands of the *NNS Framework* in England and attainment targets for *Mathematics 5–14* in Scotland to assist with your planning. You may wish to dip in and out of various Units when teaching different topics; these planning grids will help you identify easily relevant Units to support your own scheme of work.

Each Unit comprises four graded sets of exercises, A being the easiest and D being the most difficult. Also contained in each Unit is a 'Listen and Write' section, since an important aspect of developing mental skills is the ability to listen to and comprehend oral questions. The questions for you to dictate (and accompanying answers) can be found on pages 70 to 73. A further 'Think About It!' question at the end of each unit enables children to use and apply strategies learned in context.

The written activities in each Unit can be used flexibly, but should follow on from teaching of the skills and strategies being practised. You may choose to set questions:
*   during the mental/oral activity - children could be given a few minutes to complete an exercise, then answer, and strategies could be discussed as a class
*   as an independent activity - during the main part of the lesson children might be given a particular exercise to consolidate skills and strategies that have been taught
*   for homework - exercises may be given as homework for children to practise skills covered in class.

However the activities are used, it is vital to encourage children to read and use the prompts on each page, as these will support them in completing the activity. It may be useful to enlarge and display the list of key skills from pages 8 to 9 to help children internalise strategies that they will need to draw upon regularly.

After every five Units the skills covered are revisited in a Review page. These include a self-assessment 'Check-up' to help children focus on key strategies. Review pages are followed by 'Take a Break' exercises, which provide the opportunity for children to use skills in a different, less formal context. Whole-class discussion of these pages is likely to elicit the use of mathematical vocabulary and encourage children to explain the strategies used.

Learning Objectives

Unit	Topic	Learning Objectives
1	Number Facts	• Know by heart multiplication facts up to 10 x 10 and derive quickly corresponding division facts.
2	Extended Number Facts	• Use known number facts and place value to complete mental calculations.
3	Counting and Order	• Recognise and extend number sequences.
4	Measurement: Length	• Convert larger to smaller units. • Solve simple problems involving measures (length).
5	Place Value	• Read and write whole numbers in figures and words, and know what each digit represents. • Know what each digit represents in a number with up to two decimal places.
6	Number	• Know by heart all multiplication facts up to 10 x 10 and derive quickly corresponding division facts.
7	Money	• Solve problems involving money.
8	Fractions	• Use fraction notation including mixed numbers. • Relate fractions to division and use division to find simple fractions.
9	Decimals	• Relate fractions to their decimal representations. • Add or subtract decimal fractions using known number facts and place value.
10	Equations	• Use appropriate number operations to solve problems.
11	Number Facts	• Know multiplication facts up to 10 x 10 and derive quickly corresponding division facts. • Derive quickly addition and subtraction facts to 20.
12	Measurement: Time	• Convert larger to smaller units of time and vice versa. • Use units of time to solve simple problems involving time.
13	Fractions and Decimals	• Use fraction notation including mixed numbers. • Relate fractions to their decimal representations. • Relate fractions to division and use division to find simple fractions.
14	Place Value	• Read and write whole numbers in figures and words, and know what each digit represents. • Know what each digit represents in a number with up to two decimal places.
15	Doubling and Halving	• Derive quickly doubles of whole numbers 1-100, multiples of 10 to 1000, multiples of 100 to 10 000 and corresponding halves. • Use doubling and halving starting from known facts.
16	Number Facts	• Know by heart multiplication facts up to 10 x 10 and derive quickly corresponding division facts.
17	Equations	• Choose and use appropriate number operations and ways of calculating to solve number problems.
18	Measurement: Mass	• Convert larger to smaller units. • Solve problems involving measures (mass).
19	Percentages	• Express one half, one quarter, three quarters and tenths and hundredths as percentages.
20	Counting and Order	• Recognise and extend number sequences.
21	Number Facts	• Know by heart multiplication facts up to 10 x 10 and corresponding division facts. • Derive quickly addition and subtraction facts to 20.
22	Extended Number Facts	• Use known number facts and place value to calculate mentally.
23	Measurement: Capacity	• Convert larger to smaller units. • Solve simple problems involving measures (capacity).
24	Equations	• Use appropriate number operations to solve problems.
25	Counting and Order	• Recognise and extend number sequences.
26	Number Facts	• Know by heart multiplication facts to 10 x 10 and derive quickly corresponding division facts. • Derive quickly doubles of numbers to at least 100 and corresponding halves.
27	Money	• Solve problems involving money.
28	Factors	• Find all the pairs of factors of any number up to 100.
29	Fractions and Decimals	• Relate fractions to division to find simple fractions. • Express fractions as decimals or percentages.
30	Place Value	• Read and write whole numbers in figures and words and know what each digit represents. • Know what each digit represents in a number with up to two decimal places.
31	Number Facts	• Know by heart multiplication facts up to 10 x 10 and derive quickly corresponding division facts. • Derive quickly addition and subtraction facts to 20.
32	Square Numbers	• Know squares of numbers to at least 10 x 10.
33	Measurement: Time	• Solve problems involving time. • Use units of time.
34	Counting and Order	• Recognise and extend number sequences.
35	Equations	• Use appropriate number operations and ways of calculating.
36	Number Facts	• Know by heart multiplication facts up to 10 x 10 and derive quickly corresponding division facts. • Derive quickly addition and subtraction facts to 20.
37	Area and Perimeter	• Understand and use the formula for the area of a rectangle. • Understand and calculate perimeters of rectangles.
38	Fractions, Decimals, Percentages	• Change an improper fraction to a mixed number. • Relate fractions to division and use division to find simple fractions. • Use known number facts and place value for mental addition and subtraction. • Relate fractions to decimal and percentage representation.
39	Measurement	• Solve problems involving measures. • Convert larger to smaller units.
40	Terms	• Understand and use mathematical vocabulary.

National Numeracy Strategy Framework Matching Chart

Strand	Numbers and the number system			Calculations									Solving Problems			Measures, shape and space		Handling data
Topic / Unit	Place value, ordering and rounding	Properties of numbers and number sequences	Fractions, decimals and percentages, ratio and proportion	Rapid recall of addition and subtraction facts	Mental calculation strategies (+ and −)	Paper and pencil procedures (+ and −)	Understanding multiplication and division	Rapid recall of multiplication and division facts	Mental calculation strategies (× and ÷)	Paper and pencil procedures (× and ÷)	Using a calculator	Checking results of calculations	Making decisions	Reasoning and generalising about numbers or shapes	Problems involving 'real life', money or measures	Measures: Length (L), Mass (M), Capacity (C), Time (T), Area (A), Perimeter (P)	Shape and space	Organising and interpreting data
1							✓	✓	✓			✓						
2	✓			✓	✓			✓	✓									
3	✓	✓		✓	✓									✓				
4				✓	✓			✓	✓							✓	✓ (L)	
5	✓		✓	✓														
6				✓	✓		✓	✓	✓			✓						
7	✓	✓			✓				✓							✓		
8			✓	✓	✓		✓		✓									
9	✓		✓	✓	✓													
10				✓	✓		✓	✓	✓		✓	✓						
11				✓	✓		✓	✓	✓			✓						
12					✓				✓							✓	✓ (T)	
13	✓		✓	✓					✓									
14	✓		✓															
15	✓						✓	✓	✓									
16							✓	✓	✓									
17		✓		✓					✓				✓			✓		
18	✓				✓				✓							✓	✓ (M)	
19	✓		✓						✓									
20	✓	✓		✓	✓									✓				
21		✓		✓	✓		✓	✓	✓			✓						
22	✓			✓	✓			✓	✓			✓						
23	✓				✓				✓							✓	✓ (C)	
24					✓				✓			✓	✓					
25	✓	✓			✓									✓				
26		✓			✓		✓	✓	✓			✓						
27	✓			✓	✓			✓	✓							✓		
28		✓							✓									
29	✓		✓	✓					✓									
30	✓		✓	✓														
31		✓		✓	✓		✓	✓						✓				
32		✓			✓				✓									
33					✓				✓							✓	✓ (T)	
34	✓	✓									✓							
35				✓	✓			✓	✓			✓	✓					
36		✓		✓	✓			✓	✓			✓						
37					✓				✓							✓ (A & P)	✓	
38	✓	✓	✓		✓				✓									
39		✓			✓				✓		✓		✓		✓	✓ (L, C, M)		
40	✓	✓	✓		✓		✓		✓		✓	✓	✓		✓	✓ (A & P)	✓	

Mathematics 5–14 Matching Chart

Unit	Problem-solving and Enquiry	Information Handling	Range and Type of Numbers	Money	Add and Subtract	Multiply and Divide	Round Numbers	Fractions, Percentages and Ratio	Patterns and Sequences	Functions and Equations	Measure and Estimate	Time	Perimeter, Formulae and Scales	Shape, Position and Movement
1	✓					✓								
2			✓		✓	✓								
3			✓		✓				✓					
4	✓				✓	✓					✓			
5			✓		✓			✓						
6	✓				✓	✓								
7	✓		✓	✓	✓	✓	✓							
8			✓		✓	✓		✓						
9			✓		✓			✓						
10	✓				✓	✓					✓			
11	✓				✓	✓								
12	✓				✓	✓					✓	✓		
13			✓		✓	✓		✓						
14			✓					✓						
15			✓			✓								
16						✓								
17	✓		✓		✓	✓		✓			✓			
18	✓		✓	✓	✓	✓					✓			
19			✓			✓		✓						
20	✓		✓		✓				✓					
21	✓		✓		✓	✓								
22	✓		✓		✓	✓								
23	✓		✓	✓	✓	✓					✓			
24	✓				✓	✓					✓			
25	✓		✓		✓				✓					
26	✓		✓		✓	✓								
27	✓		✓	✓	✓	✓	✓							
28			✓			✓			✓	✓				
29			✓		✓	✓		✓						
30			✓		✓			✓						
31	✓		✓		✓	✓			✓					
32			✓		✓	✓			✓					
33	✓				✓	✓					✓	✓		
34	✓		✓	✓	✓				✓					
35	✓			✓	✓	✓					✓			
36	✓		✓		✓	✓					✓			
37					✓	✓					✓		✓	✓
38			✓		✓	✓		✓						
39	✓		✓	✓	✓	✓					✓			
40	✓		✓	✓	✓	✓		✓		✓	✓		✓	✓

Mental Skills and Strategies

Number Facts

1. When you add (a positive number) or multiply (by a whole number greater than 1) the answer will be more.

2. When you subtract (a positive number) or divide (by a whole number greater than 1) the answer will be less.

3. Round up or down to make an estimate and check your answer is reasonable.

4. Check using the inverse operation.

    addition ⟷ subtraction
    multiplication ⟷ division

5. Use knowledge of the sum, difference and product of odd and even numbers.

    O + O = E   O − O = E
    E + E = E   E − E = E
    O + E = O   O − E = O
    E + O = O   E − O = O
    O × O = O   E × E = E
    O × E = E   E × O = E

6. Learn doubles and corresponding halves: two-digit numbers, e.g. 3.5×2, 0.53×2, multiples of 10 to 1000, multiples of 100 to 10 000.

7. Use bridging facts, e.g. $0.8 + 0.7 = 0.8 + 0.2 + 0.5$.

8. Use known facts to extend to new facts, e.g. $9 + 6 = 15$ so $7.9 + 0.6 = 8.5$.

9. Make tens to help with addition. $47 + 17$ is the same as $50 + 14$ or $44 + 20$.

10. Make tens to help with subtraction. $79 − 13$ is the same as $80 − 14$ or $76 − 10$.

11. Find the difference by counting up through the next multiple of 10, 100, 1000, e.g. $3017 − 2898$, 2 to 2900, 100 more to 3000, 17 more to 3017, difference of 119.

12. Learn square numbers up to 10×10 and squares of multiples of 10, e.g. $20 \times 20 = 400$.

13. Learn laws of divisibility:

    - If the last digit is even, the number is divisible by 2.
    - If the last digit is 0 or 5, the number is divisible by 5.
    - If the last digit is 0, the number is divisible by 2, 5 and 10.
    - If the last 2 digits are 0s, the number is divisible by 100.
    - If the last 2 digits are divisible by 4, the number is divisible by 4.

14. Find pairs of factors to 100. A pair of factors will multiply together to make a given product, e.g. 2 and 3 are a factor pair of 6; 5 and 7 are a factor pair of 35.

15. When multiplying by 10, 100 or 1000 move the digits the number of zeros to the left.

16. When dividing by 10, 100 or 1000 move the digits the number of zeros to the right.

17. Partition to divide, e.g. $248 \div 4 = (200 \div 4) + (40 \div 4) + (8 \div 4) = 50 + 10 + 2 = 62$.

Mental Skills and Strategies

Fractions, Decimals and Percentages

18 If the top number is smaller than the bottom number, the fraction must be less than 1.

19 When multiplying a fraction (less than 1) by a whole number, the answer will be smaller than the whole number.

20 Try changing fractions to decimals to make computations easier.

21 If the numerator and the denominator are of the same value, the fraction = 1.

22 In an improper fraction, the numerator is greater than the denominator.

23 A mixed number is a whole number and a common fraction.

24 To find an equivalent fraction multiply or divide the numerator and denominator by the same number.

25 % means out of 100.

26 To find 10% ÷ by 10
20% is double 10%
5% is half of 10%
50% = $\frac{1}{2}$

Measurement and Money

27 Make all units of measurement the same when solving problems involving measures.

28 To change minutes to hours and minutes divide by 60. To change seconds to minutes and seconds divide by 60.

29 To change days to hours multiply by 24.

30 Area of a rectangle = length × breadth.

31 Perimeter = sum of all side lengths.

32 Use language clues:

- *centi* = 100 (100 centimetres = 1 metre)
- *milli* = 1000 (1000 millilitre = 1 litre)

UNIT 1 Number Facts

- use a known fact and addition or subtraction (e.g. 6 × 7 = 5 × 7 + one more 7)
- use commutative law (e.g. 5 × 8 is the same as 8 × 5)
- multiplication is repeated addition
- division is repeated subtraction
- use inverse operations (e.g. ____ ÷ 4 = 6; 6 × 4 = 24)

A Complete.

× means the answer will be more.

1. 3 × 4 = _____
2. 6 × 5 = _____
3. 24 ÷ 3 = _____
4. 5 × 8 = _____
5. 45 ÷ 9 = _____
6. 27 ÷ 3 = _____
7. 9 × 2 = _____
8. 24 ÷ 2 = _____
9. _____ ÷ 3 = 6
10. _____ × 5 = 20

→ Score

B Complete.

1. 7 × 10 = _____
2. 2 × 6 = _____
3. 15 ÷ 3 = _____
4. 40 ÷ 8 = _____
5. 9 × 4 = _____
6. 16 ÷ 4 = _____
7. _____ ÷ 10 = 5
8. _____ × 4 = 32
9. _____ ÷ 4 = 7
10. _____ × 3 = 21

→ Score

C Complete.

÷ means the answer will be less.

1. 7 × 4 = _____
2. 6 × 6 = _____
3. 100 ÷ 10 = _____
4. 48 ÷ 6 = _____
5. 8 × 10 = _____
6. 20 ÷ 4 = _____
7. _____ ÷ 6 = 9
8. _____ × 3 = 12
9. _____ ÷ 6 = 5
10. _____ × 4 = 36

→ Score

D Complete.

Try rearranging. 56 ÷ 8? so 8 × ? = 56.

1. 7 × 7 = _____
2. 56 ÷ 8 = _____
3. 4 × 9 = _____
4. 42 ÷ 7 = _____
5. 8 × 8 = _____
6. 8 × 9 = _____
7. _____ × 7 = 35
8. _____ ÷ 9 = 9
9. _____ × 8 = 48
10. _____ ÷ 8 = 3

→ Score

Listen and Write

1. _____   6. _____
2. _____   7. _____
3. _____   8. _____
4. _____   9. _____
5. _____   10. _____

→ Score

Think About It!

WonderGal's bill
7 Invisi Tablets @ £6 each
4 Nukem Bars @ £7 each

SoupaGuy's bill
8 Energy Pills @ £4 each
4 Time Transporter Eggs @ £5 each

Batboy's bill
9 Atom Blastas @ £3 each
½ dozen Krypto Bars @ £3 each

Ribbon's bill
5 Memory Munchies @ £8 each
2 Sonic Crunchers @ £9 each

Who paid the most at the SoupaMarket? _____

- Know by heart multiplication facts up to 10 × 10 and derive quickly corresponding division facts.

10

© OUP: Copying permitted for purchasing school only.

UNIT 2 — Extended Number Facts

Strategies
- when multiplying by 10s move digits one place to left
- when multiplying by 100s move digits two places to left
- move digits to right when you divide by 10
- use knowledge of basic number facts (e.g. 8 + 9, 6 + 7, doubles, etc.)

A Complete.
1. 18 + 7 = _____
2. 38 + 7 = _____
3. 15 − 6 = _____
4. 45 − 6 = _____
5. 600 + _____ = 824
6. 600 ÷ 3 = _____
7. 600 ÷ 30 = _____
8. _____ × 200 = 800
9. 400 ÷ 4 = _____
10. 20 × 10 = _____

→ Score

B Complete.
1. 29 + 5 = _____
2. 69 + 5 = _____
3. 21 − 8 = _____
4. 51 − 8 = _____
5. 958 − _____ = 658
6. 900 ÷ 10 = _____
7. 900 ÷ 100 = _____
8. _____ × 300 = 900
9. 800 ÷ 4 = _____
10. 51 × 10 = _____

→ Score

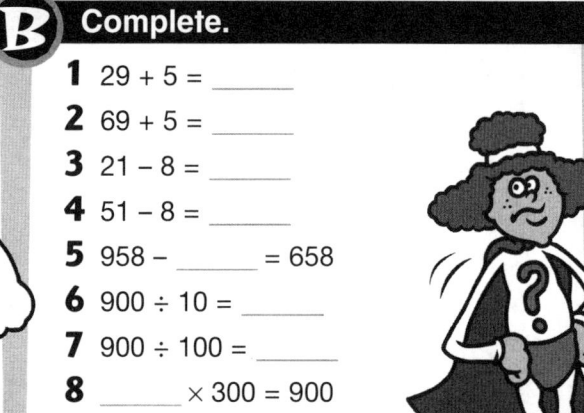

C Complete.
1. 36 + 9 = _____
2. 76 + 9 = _____
3. 32 − 8 = _____
4. 52 − 8 = _____
5. _____ + 215 = 515
6. 80 × 9 = _____
7. 800 × 9 = _____
8. _____ × 400 = 3200
9. 320 ÷ 4 = _____
10. 68 × 10 = _____

Drop the zeros. Multiply or divide. Add the zeros to your answer.

→ Score

D Complete.
1. 27 + 4 = _____
2. 87 + 4 = _____
3. 23 − 7 = _____
4. 73 − 7 = _____
5. _____ − 400 = 329
6. 60 × 7 = _____
7. 600 × 7 = _____
8. _____ × 500 = 2000
9. 320 ÷ 40 = _____
10. 73 × 10 = _____

Use the basic number facts you already know to help. 7 + 4   13 − 7

→ Score

Listen and Write
1. _____   6. _____
2. _____   7. _____
3. _____   8. _____
4. _____   9. _____
5. _____   10. _____

→ Score

Think About It!
In 60 games of SOUPABALL Batboy has scored a total of 1200 hits.

What is Batboy's hitting average? _____

Clue: Total hits divided by number of games equals average.

Learning objective
- Use known number facts and place value to complete mental calculations.

11

© OUP: Copying permitted for purchasing school only.

UNIT 3 Counting and Order

Strategies
- try calculating the difference between consecutive numbers (e.g. 925, 932, 939   939 − 932 = 7   932 − 925 = 7)
- ask, 'Which digits repeat or change?'
- ask, 'Am I counting forwards or backwards?'
- ask, 'Could there be more than one operation in the counting pattern?'

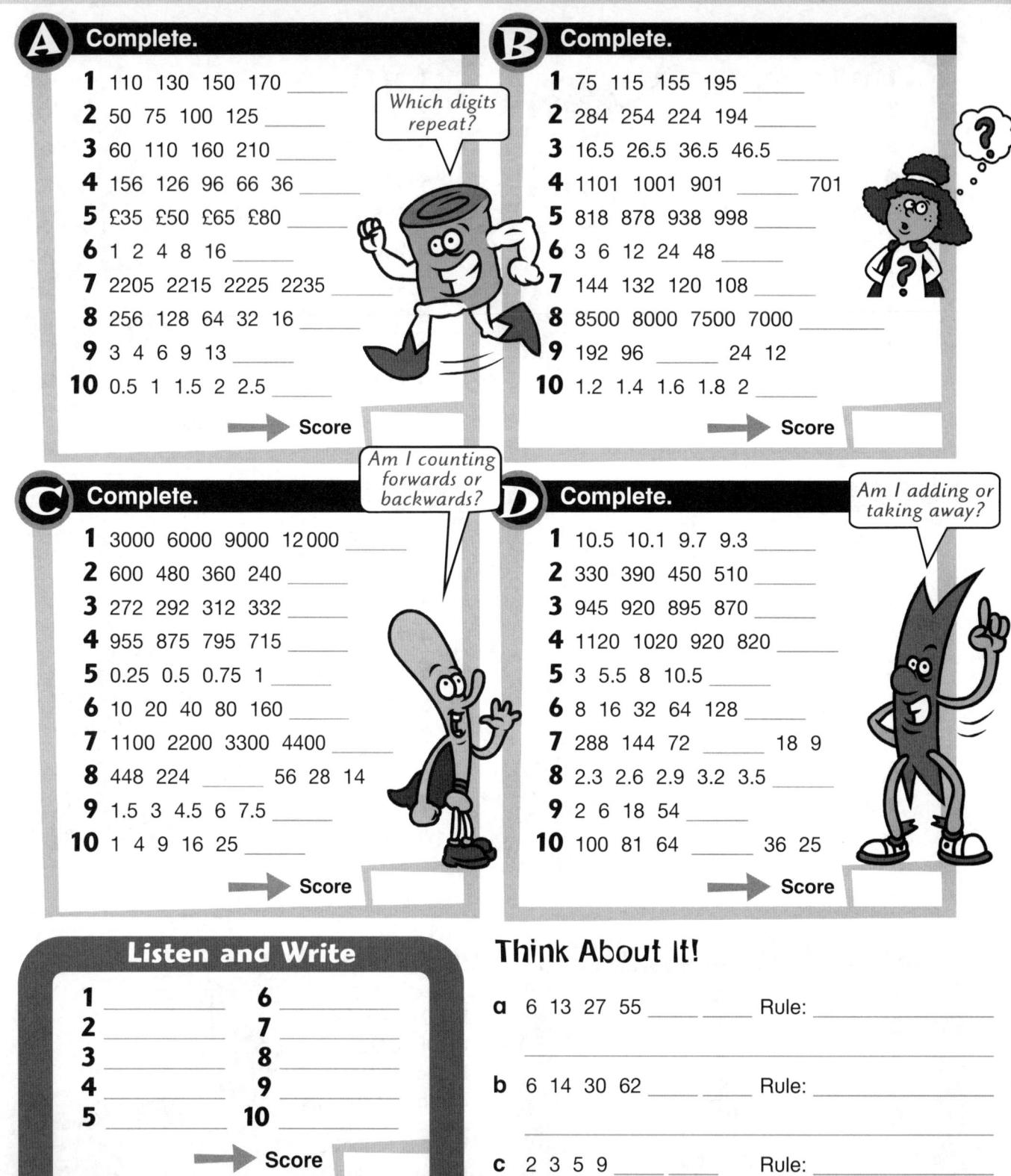

A Complete.
1. 110 130 150 170 _____
2. 50 75 100 125 _____
3. 60 110 160 210 _____
4. 156 126 96 66 36 _____
5. £35 £50 £65 £80 _____
6. 1 2 4 8 16 _____
7. 2205 2215 2225 2235 _____
8. 256 128 64 32 16 _____
9. 3 4 6 9 13 _____
10. 0.5 1 1.5 2 2.5 _____

Which digits repeat?

Score ____

B Complete.
1. 75 115 155 195 _____
2. 284 254 224 194 _____
3. 16.5 26.5 36.5 46.5 _____
4. 1101 1001 901 _____ 701
5. 818 878 938 998 _____
6. 3 6 12 24 48 _____
7. 144 132 120 108 _____
8. 8500 8000 7500 7000 _____
9. 192 96 _____ 24 12
10. 1.2 1.4 1.6 1.8 2 _____

Score ____

C Complete.
1. 3000 6000 9000 12 000 _____
2. 600 480 360 240 _____
3. 272 292 312 332 _____
4. 955 875 795 715 _____
5. 0.25 0.5 0.75 1 _____
6. 10 20 40 80 160 _____
7. 1100 2200 3300 4400 _____
8. 448 224 _____ 56 28 14
9. 1.5 3 4.5 6 7.5 _____
10. 1 4 9 16 25 _____

Am I counting forwards or backwards?

Score ____

D Complete.
1. 10.5 10.1 9.7 9.3 _____
2. 330 390 450 510 _____
3. 945 920 895 870 _____
4. 1120 1020 920 820 _____
5. 3 5.5 8 10.5 _____
6. 8 16 32 64 128 _____
7. 288 144 72 _____ 18 9
8. 2.3 2.6 2.9 3.2 3.5 _____
9. 2 6 18 54 _____
10. 100 81 64 _____ 36 25

Am I adding or taking away?

Score ____

Listen and Write
1. ____   6. ____
2. ____   7. ____
3. ____   8. ____
4. ____   9. ____
5. ____   10. ____

Score ____

Think About It!

a   6 13 27 55 ____ ____   Rule: _____

b   6 14 30 62 ____ ____   Rule: _____

c   2 3 5 9 ____ ____   Rule: _____

Learning objective
- Recognise and extend number sequences.

© OUP: Copying permitted for purchasing school only.

Unit 4 — Measurement: Length

Strategies
- use knowledge of basic number facts
- change to common units
- ask, 'Will the answer be more (+ and ×) or less (− and ÷)?'
- learn and use measurement tables

A Complete.

1. 8 cm + 6 cm + 9 cm + 7 cm = _____ cm
2. 8.7 m − 4.3 m = _____ m
3. Metres in 500 cm? _____ m
4. 2.5 m + 2.5 m = _____ m
5. 25 cm × 4 = _____
6. 300 cm ÷ 6 = _____ cm
7. 2 metres = _____ cm
8. 8 m + 24 cm = _____ cm
9. 6.75 m − 4 m = _____ m
10. 8000 mm = _____ m

→ Score

B Complete.

Remember: 100 cm = 1 metre.

1. 9 mm + 4 mm + 7 mm + 8 mm = _____ mm
2. 6.9 m − 3.6 m = _____ m
3. Metres in 3 km? _____ m
4. 1.5 m + 3.5 m = _____ m
5. 476 cm = _____ m _____ cm
6. 500 m ÷ 50 = _____ m
7. 1 cm = _____ mm
8. 4 km + 246 m = _____ m
9. 855 cm − 2 m = _____ cm
10. 120 mm × 4 = _____

→ Score

C Complete.

Remember: 1000 m = 1 kilometre.

1. 5.6 m + 3.7 m = _____ m
2. 5.1 m − 2.4 m = _____ m
3. Centimetres in 2.6 m? _____ cm
4. 2.5 cm + 3.5 cm = _____ cm
5. 70 m × 4 = _____
6. 6295 m = _____ km _____ m
7. Metres in 1.5 km? _____ m
8. 6500 m − 1.2 km = _____ m
9. 6 cm + 7 mm = _____ mm
10. 800 mm ÷ 40 = _____ mm

→ Score

D Complete.

Remember: 1000 mm = 1 metre.

1. 12.75 m + 8.04 m = _____ m
2. 9 m − 3.8 m = _____ m
3. Millimetres in 1.2 m? _____ mm
4. 4.5 mm + 5.1 mm = _____ mm
5. 30 cm × 8 = _____ m _____ cm
6. 38 mm = _____ cm _____ mm
7. 2.8 cm + 76 mm = _____ mm
8. 250 m + 2.5 km + 100 m = _____ km
9. Metres in 4.8 km? _____
10. 900 km ÷ 50 = _____ km

→ Score

Listen and Write

1. _____   6. _____
2. _____   7. _____
3. _____   8. _____
4. _____   9. _____
5. _____   10. _____

→ Score

Think About It!

Who won the SoupaAths high jump competition?

- SoupaGuy jumped 32 metres 20 cm.
- Batboy jumped 3020 metres.
- WonderGal jumped 3.2 km.
- Ribbon jumped 3200 cm.

The winner was _____

Learning objectives
- Convert larger to smaller units.
- Solve simple problems involving measures (length).

© OUP: Copying permitted for purchasing school only.

UNIT 5 Place Value

Strategies
- zero holds a place
- in any number the value of a digit is determined by the place it occupies
- remember the Place Value chart

millions	thousands	units
h t u	h t u	h t u

A Complete.

1. 6000 + 700 + 30 + 4 = _____
2. 8 + 4000 + 70 = _____
3. 3926 = _____ hundreds + 26 units
4. 3590 = _____ + 90 + 3000
5. Value of 8 in 5438? _____
6. 7.5 = 7 units + _____ tenths
7. Value of 3 in 80 235? _____
8. 165.4 = 16 tens + 5 units + _____ tenths
9. Value of 3 in 2.3? _____
10. Value of 15 in 157? _____

→ Score

B Complete.

1. 60 000 + 400 + 20 + 8 = _____
2. 500 + 50 000 + 5 = _____
3. 8435 = _____ tens + 5 units
4. 32 030 = _____ + 20 + 2000
5. Value of 6 in 16 821? _____
6. 26.4 = 2 tens + 6 units + _____
7. Value of 4 in 1.04? _____
8. Value of 5 in 72 954? _____
9. Value of 37 in 4137? _____
10. 264.3 = $\frac{3}{10}$ + 200 + 4 + _____

→ Score

10 tens = 100
10 hundreds = 1000

C Complete.

1. 80 000 + 80 + 8 = _____
2. 6 + 700 + 20 000 + 4000 = _____
3. 7694 = 7 thousands + _____ units
4. 88 900 = 900 + 80 000 + _____
5. Value of 9 in 79 653? _____
6. 3.21 = 3 units + 2 tenths + _____ hundredths
7. Value of 5 in 482.5? _____
8. Value of 2 in 273 941? _____
9. Value of 24 in 5243? _____
10. 492.35 = 400 + 90 + 2 + _____

→ Score

D Complete.

1. 600 000 + 50 000 + 4000 + 800 + 50 = _____
2. 100 + 100 000 + 1 = _____
3. 49 052 = _____ hundreds + 52 units
4. 780 060 = 700 000 + _____ + 60
5. Value of 4 in 24 382? _____
6. 15.64 = 15 units + _____ hundredths
7. Value of 9 in 8086.49? _____
8. Value of 6 in 568 904? _____
9. Value of 76 in 84 769? _____
10. 765.02 = 76 tens 5 units _____

→ Score

Listen and Write

1. _____   6. _____
2. _____   7. _____
3. _____   8. _____
4. _____   9. _____
5. _____   10. _____

→ Score

Think About It!

Use the clues and your knowledge of place value to identify the number.

- I am a 5-digit number.
- My middle digit is even.
- My first and last digits are odd.
- No digit is repeated.
- My ten thousands digit is 4 less than my units digit.
- The digits in my thousands, hundreds and tens places are consecutive.

I am _____

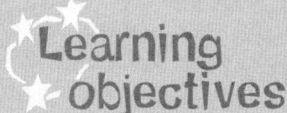

Learning objectives
- Read and write whole numbers in figures and words, and know what each digit represents.
- Know what each digit represents in a number with up to two decimal places.

Review   1

A Complete.

1. 9 × 8 = _____
2. 56 ÷ 7 = _____
3. _____ × 5 = 30
4. 24 ÷ _____ = 4
5. Next? 327 407 487 _____
6. 600 + _____ = 937
7. Value of 6 in 8643? _____
8. metres in 5.5 km? _____ m
9. 5.25 km + 440 m = _____
10. 650 km ÷ 50 = _____

→ Score

B Complete.

1. 7 × 6 = _____
2. 64 ÷ 8 = _____
3. _____ × 8 = 48
4. 35 ÷ _____ = 7
5. Next? 1990 1790 1590 _____
6. 784 – _____ = 384
7. Value of 5 in 52 973? _____
8. centimetres in 2.4 m? _____ cm
9. 8.75 km – 300 m = _____
10. 7 × 40 km = _____

→ Score

C Complete.

1. 8 × 7 = _____
2. 72 ÷ 8 - _____
3. _____ × 4 = 36
4. 24 ÷ _____ = 3
5. Next? 5.3 5.6 5.9 _____
6. _____ × 300 = 1200
7. Value of 2 in 12 478? _____
8. millimetres in 58 cm? _____ mm
9. 6 × 150 cm = _____ m
10. 15 cm × 10 = _____ m

→ Score

D Complete.

1. 9 × 9 = _____
2. 49 ÷ 7 = _____
3. _____ × 7 = 28
4. 48 ÷ _____ = 8
5. Next? 28.75 28.50 28.25 _____
6. 1600 ÷ 4 = _____
7. Value of 3 in 357 206? _____
8. mm in 1.2 metres? _____ mm
9. 1500 mm ÷ 3 = _____ mm
10. 800 mm ÷ 4 = _____ mm

→ Score

Listen and Write

1. _____   6. _____
2. _____   7. _____
3. _____   8. _____
4. _____   9. _____
5. _____ 10. _____

→ Score

Think About It!

Use the clues to identify the numbers on Ribbon's cards.

1. The numbers are not the same.
2. Their product is greater than 60 but less than 65.
3. The sum of the numbers is 16.

 Check-up
- I know multiplication facts up to 10 × 10.
- I can extend number sequences that increase or decrease by a constant amount.
- I know the value of each digit in whole numbers to 1 million.

15

© OUP: Copying permitted for purchasing school only.

Take a Break 1

SoupaHeroes to the rescue!

Help the SoupaHeroes carry out their good deeds for the day by completing the equations in their rescue paths.

Time each SoupaHero's rescue attempt!

SoupaGuy

$3 \times 8 =$ _____

$48 \div 6 =$ _____

$17 + 6 + 9 =$ _____

$73 - 9 =$ _____

$5 \times 8 + 5 =$ _____

Value of 7 in 178 294? _____

8.5 cm − 2 mm = _____ mm

Next?
5 10 20 40
_____

Stopped the bank from being robbed.

Time: _____

WonderGal

$4 \times 9 =$ _____

$27 \div 3 =$ _____

$28 + 6 + 9 =$ _____

$37 + 5 + 4 =$ _____

$63 - 8 =$ _____

$4 \times 6 + 8 =$ _____

Value of 8 in 286 534? _____

6.8 cm − 9 mm = _____ mm

Next?
256 128 64 32
_____

Saved the crew of a sinking ship.

Time: _____

Batboy

$7 \times 6 =$ _____

$54 \div 9 =$ _____

$54 - 9 =$ _____

$7 \times 3 + 9 =$ _____

Value of 9 in 178 294?
_____

7.4 cm + 9 mm = _____ mm

Next? 4 9 16 25
_____

Rescued a kidnapped princess.

Time: _____

Ribbon

$9 \times 8 =$ _____

$28 \div 4 =$ _____

$8 + 16 + 9 =$ _____

$82 - 8 =$ _____

$5 \times 4 + 6 =$ _____

Value of 6 in 653 790?
_____

3.2 cm minus 8 mm equals
_____

Next?
1.5 3 4.5 6
_____

Saved a crashing plane.

Time: _____

Learning objective

- Use known number facts, place value, knowledge of units of length and extending number sequences.

UNIT 6 Number Facts

- multiplication is repeated addition and division is repeated subtraction
- A × B is the same as B × A (commutative law)
- A ÷ B = C is the same as C × B = A (inverse operation)
- ask, 'Can I partition?' (e.g. 8 × 7 is the same as 5 × 7 + 3 × 7) (distributive law)

Strategies

A Complete.

1. 6 × 7 = _____
2. 9 × 5 = _____
3. 15 ÷ 3 = _____
4. 7 × 7 = _____
5. 25 ÷ 5 = _____
6. 3 × __ = 24
7. 4 × 8 = _____
8. _____ ÷ 8 = 6
9. _____ × 9 = 27
10. 40 ÷ _____ = 8

→ Score

Remember: multiplying means that the answer will be more.

B Complete.

1. 8 × 4 = _____
2. 9 × 7 = _____
3. 54 ÷ 6 = _____
4. square 5 = _____
5. 72 ÷ 8 = _____
6. 6 × _____ = 18
7. Product of 7 and 10? _____
8. _____ ÷ 4 = 9
9. _____ × 5 = 35
10. 84 ÷ _____ = 21

→ Score

When you square a number you multiply it by itself.

C Complete.

1. 6 × 9 = _____
2. 7 × 10 = _____
3. 24 ÷ 8 = _____
4. square 8 = _____
5. 49 ÷ 7 = _____
6. 8 × _____ = 64
7. Product of 8 and 4? _____
8. _____ ÷ 6 = 7
9. _____ × 4 = 48
10. 18 ÷ _____ = 6

→ Score

D Complete.

1. 8 × 9 = _____
2. 6 × 8 = _____
3. 36 ÷ 6 = _____
4. square 10 = _____
5. 32 ÷ 4 = _____
6. 7 × _____ = 63
7. Product of 9 and 6? _____
8. _____ ÷ 8 = 7
9. _____ × 5 = 55
10. 28 ÷ _____ = 4

→ Score

Remember: dividing means that the answer will be less.

Listen and Write

1. _____   6. _____
2. _____   7. _____
3. _____   8. _____
4. _____   9. _____
5. _____   10. _____

→ Score

Think About It!

Can you finish solving SoupaGuy's Y pattern and then write the rule he has used?

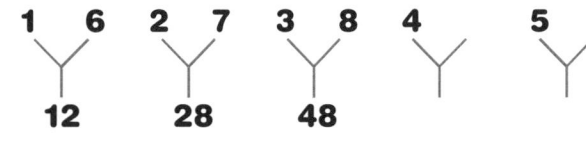

Learning objective

- Know by heart all multiplication facts up to 10 × 10 and derive quickly corresponding division facts.

© OUP: Copying permitted for purchasing school only.

UNIT 7 Money

Strategies
- estimate an answer
- round up or down
- use known basic number facts
- count on

To find change: count on.

A Complete.
1. £1 – 5p = _____
2. £2, how many 10 pence coins? _____
3. Pence in £1.57? _____
4. Change from £1 if I spend 55p? _____
5. £5.45 + £3.40 = _____
6. 4 note pads @ 25p each? _____
7. 50p, how many 5 pence coins? _____
8. Spent £1.95. Change from £2? _____
9. $\frac{1}{4}$ of £20 = _____
10. 3 kg @ 60p a kg? _____

→ Score _____

B Complete.
1. £1 – 25p = _____
2. £2, how many 50 pence coins? _____
3. Pence in £2.45? _____
4. Change from £1 if I spend 69p? _____
5. 9 metres @ 50p a metre? _____
6. 10 pencils @ 20p each? _____
7. £1, how many 5 pence coins? _____
8. Spent £1.69. Change from £2? _____
9. $\frac{1}{4}$ of £16 = _____
10. £5 – £1.75 = _____

→ Score _____

C Complete.
1. £1 – 15p = _____
2. £2, how many 5 pence coins? _____
3. Pence in £5? _____
4. Change from £2 if I spend 78p? _____
5. 4 × £3.50 = _____
6. 6 balls @ 15p each? _____
7. £2, how many 20p coins? _____
8. Spent £1.55. Change from £5? _____
9. $\frac{1}{4}$ of £1.60 = _____
10. 500 g @ £10 a kg? _____

→ Score _____

D Complete.
1. £1 – 49p = _____
2. £5, how many 20 pence coins? _____
3. Pence in £7.50? _____
4. Change from £5 if I spend £3.20? _____
5. £2.50 ÷ 5 = _____
6. 8 ice-pops @ 80p each? _____
7. £5, how many 10p coins? _____
8. Spent £7.95. Change from £10? _____
9. $\frac{1}{4}$ of £50 = _____
10. 250 kg @ £8 a kg? _____

→ Score _____

Remember: @ means at.

Listen and Write
1 _____ 6 _____
2 _____ 7 _____
3 _____ 8 _____
4 _____ 9 _____
5 _____ 10 _____

→ Score _____

Think About It!
Make up this SoupaBill.

500 g SoupaCheese @ £1.80 a kg _____
2 kg WundaSugar @ 30p a kg _____
2 loaves of MarvelBread @ 45p a loaf _____
250 g PowerFlour @ £2.40 a kg _____

Total _____

Learning objective
- Solve problems involving money.

UNIT 8 Fractions

Strategies
- common fraction × whole number: top number × whole number ÷ denominator
- common fraction + or − common fraction: change to equivalents then add or subtract numerators (denominators stay the same)
- mixed number + or − mixed number: add or subtract whole numbers then add or subtract common fractions (as above)

A Complete.

1. $\frac{1}{2}$ of 10 = _____
2. $\frac{1}{2}$ of 24 = _____
3. $\frac{1}{4}$ of 12 = _____
4. $\frac{1}{4}$ of 16 = _____
5. $\frac{1}{4}$ of 20 = _____
6. $\frac{1}{3}$ of 9 = _____
7. $\frac{1}{5}$ of 15 = _____
8. $\frac{1}{3}$ of 12 = _____
9. $\frac{1}{10}$ of 40 = _____
10. $\frac{1}{4}$ of 24 = _____

The top number of a common fraction is smaller than the bottom number.

→ Score

B Complete.

1. $\frac{1}{3}$ of 18 = _____
2. $\frac{1}{5}$ of 20 = _____
3. $\frac{1}{3} + \frac{1}{3}$ = _____
4. $\frac{1}{4} + \frac{1}{4}$ = _____
5. $\frac{2}{4} + \frac{1}{4}$ = _____
6. $\frac{1}{4} + \frac{3}{4}$ = _____
7. $\frac{2}{4} - \frac{1}{4}$ = _____
8. $\frac{3}{4} - \frac{2}{4}$ = _____
9. $\frac{2}{3} - \frac{1}{3}$ = _____
10. $\frac{3}{5} - \frac{1}{5}$ = _____

If you change the denominator don't forget to change the numerator too!

→ Score

C Complete.

1. $\frac{1}{2}$ of 3 = _____
2. $\frac{1}{6} + \frac{1}{6}$ = _____
3. $\frac{1}{3}$ of 15 = _____
4. $\frac{2}{6} + \frac{1}{6}$ = _____
5. $\frac{2}{6} - \frac{1}{6}$ = _____
6. $\frac{2}{10} - \frac{1}{10}$ = _____
7. $\frac{1}{2} + \frac{1}{4} + \frac{1}{4}$ = _____
8. $\frac{1}{2} + \frac{3}{4}$ = _____
9. $\frac{1}{8}$ of 24 = _____
10. $\frac{1}{9}$ of 18 = _____

I wonder what a numerator and a denominator are?

→ Score

D Complete.

1. $\frac{3}{4}$ of 12 = _____
2. $\frac{2}{5}$ of 20 = _____
3. $1\frac{1}{4} + 1\frac{1}{4}$ = _____
4. $3\frac{1}{4} - 1\frac{1}{4}$ = _____
5. $\frac{7}{8}$ of 24 = _____
6. $\frac{5}{6}$ of 30 = _____
7. $4\frac{3}{8} - 2\frac{1}{8}$ = _____
8. $2\frac{1}{5} + 1\frac{1}{5} + 2\frac{4}{5}$ = _____
9. $\frac{1}{8} + \frac{3}{8} + \frac{1}{2}$ = _____
10. $\frac{1}{3} + \frac{2}{3} + \frac{1}{3}$ = _____

That's easy... numerator = top number denominator = bottom number.

→ Score

Listen and Write

1 _____   6 _____
2 _____   7 _____
3 _____   8 _____
4 _____   9 _____
5 _____   10 _____

→ Score

Think About It!

The SoupaPizza was cut into 12 even pieces.
- SoupaGuy ate $\frac{1}{3}$ of the pizza.
- WonderGal ate $\frac{1}{6}$.
- Batboy ate $\frac{1}{4}$.

How many pieces were left for Ribbon? _____

Learning objectives
- Use fraction notation including mixed numbers.
- Relate fractions to division and use division to find simple fractions.

19

© OUP: Copying permitted for purchasing school only.

UNIT 9 Decimals

Strategies
- change the denominator of the fraction to tenths or hundredths
- the number to the right of the decimal point is the numerator of the fraction
- the number to the left of the decimal point must be a whole number
- the number to the right of the decimal point must be less than 1

A Write as decimals.

1. $\frac{1}{10}$ = _____
2. $\frac{7}{10}$ = _____
3. $\frac{1}{2}$ = _____
4. $\frac{3}{10}$ = _____
5. $\frac{1}{5}$ = _____
6. $\frac{9}{10}$ = _____
7. $2\frac{1}{10}$ = _____
8. $3\frac{1}{2}$ = _____
9. $4\frac{7}{10}$ = _____
10. $1\frac{1}{5}$ = _____

Remember: $\frac{1}{10}$ = 0.1

→ Score

B Write as fractions.

1. 0.5 = _____
2. 0.1 = _____
3. 0.4 = _____
4. 1.1 = _____
5. 2.7 = _____
6. 8.5 = _____
7. 5.9 = _____
8. 0.25 = _____
9. 7.25 = _____
10. 0.75 = _____

Remember: $\frac{1}{100}$ = 0.01

→ Score

C Write answers as decimals.

1. 0.7 + 0.2 = _____
2. 0.3 + 0.4 = _____
3. $\frac{1}{4}$ = _____
4. 0.6 + 0.7 = _____
5. 0.9 − 0.3 = _____
6. 1.5 + 1.5 + 0.5 = _____
7. $\frac{3}{4}$ = _____
8. 0.8 + 3.3 = _____
9. 0.8 − 0.4 = _____
10. $5\frac{1}{4} + 2\frac{1}{2}$ = _____

If I can't change the fraction to tenths I wonder if I can change it to hundredths?

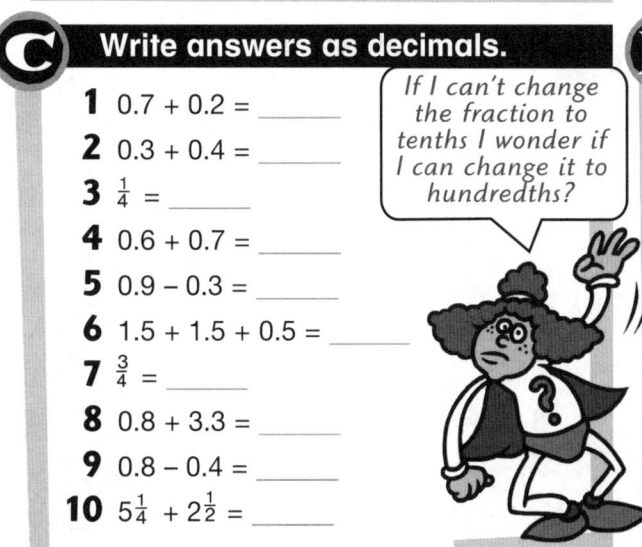

→ Score

D Write answers as fractions.

1. 0.25 + 0.25 = _____
2. 0.5 + 0.2 = _____
3. 1.4 − 0.8 = _____
4. 3.3 + 2.1 = _____
5. 1.25 + 2.25 = _____
6. 6.8 − 4.5 = _____
7. 1.5 + 2.25 = _____
8. 1.8 − 0.7 = _____
9. 2.9 − 0.4 = _____
10. 6.5 − 1.25 = _____

Add or subtract and then change to a common fraction.

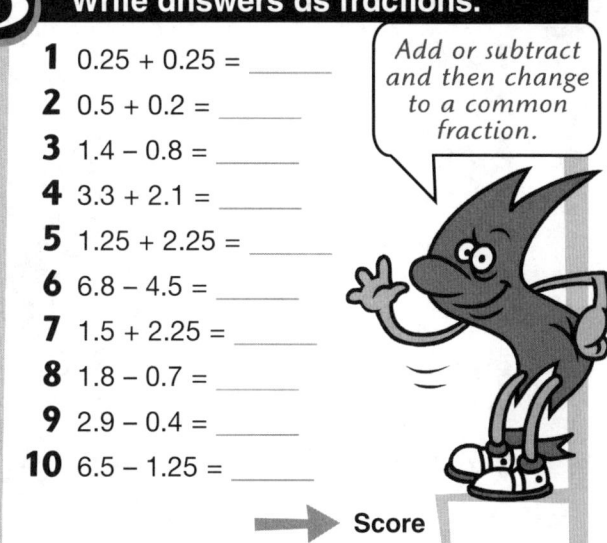

→ Score

Listen and Write

1 _____   6 _____
2 _____   7 _____
3 _____   8 _____
4 _____   9 _____
5 _____   10 _____

→ Score

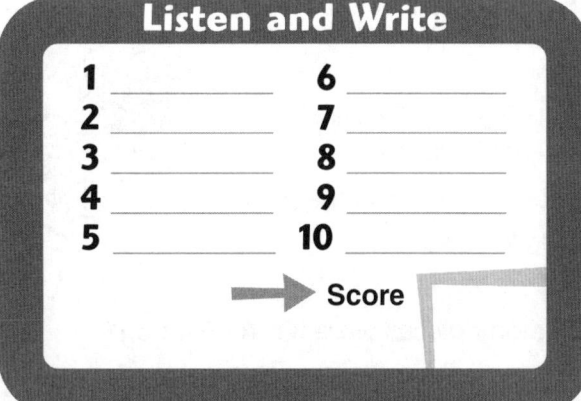

Think About It!

At the SoupaAths:

SoupaGuy jumped 0.3 km.
Batboy jumped $\frac{1}{2}$ a km.
WonderGal jumped 750 metres.
Ribbon jumped 0.5 km but was penalised $\frac{1}{10}$ of a km.

Write the results.

1st _____ distance _____   2nd _____ distance _____
3rd _____ distance _____   4th _____ distance _____

Learning objectives
- Relate fractions to their decimal representations.
- Add or subtract decimal fractions using known number facts and place value.

20

© OUP: Copying permitted for purchasing school only.

UNIT **10**

Equations

Strategies

- *both sides of = should be the same*
- *work out the brackets first then × and ÷ and then + and –*
- *ask, 'Have numbers been partitioned?'*

A Complete.

1 6 + ____ = 15
2 ____ + 8 = 17
3 24 – ____ = 16
4 ____ – 9 = 17
5 5 × ____ = 8 × 5
6 10 × 7 = ____ × 7 + ____ × 7
7 55 + 78 = 50 + ____ + 13
8 (8 × ____) + 7 = 23
9 (7 × 9) – ____ = 53
10 (54 ÷ ____) + 10 = 19

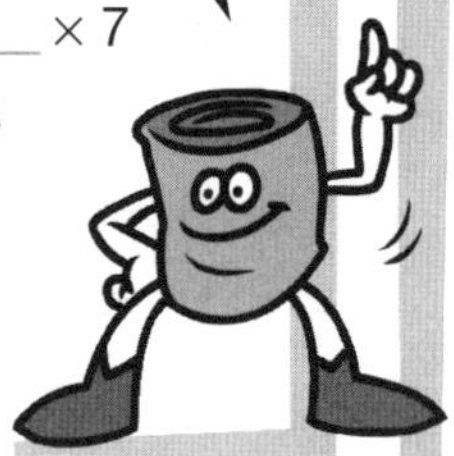

Remember: one side of the = sign must be the same as the other.

Score

B Complete.

Try working backwards.

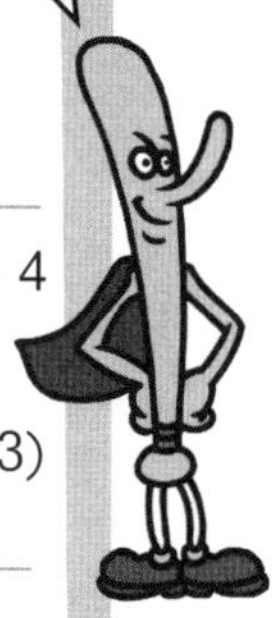

1 ____ + 26 = 35
2 ____ – 8 = 46
3 3×16 = (3× ____) + (3× ____) = ____
4 84 ÷ 4 = 40 ÷ 4 + ____ ÷ 4 + ____ ÷ 4
5 (9 × ____) + 5 = 68
6 7+7+7+8+8+8 = (7× ____)+(____ ×3)
7 36 × 5 = (____ × 5) + (____ × 5) = ____
8 7 × (15 + 9) = 7 × ____ + 7 × ____
9 (28 + 12) ÷ ____ = 4
10 4 × 800 = ____ × 400

Score

C Complete.

1 (8 × ____) + 16 = 56
2 (4 × 6) + (4 × 4) = 4 × ____
3 (52 + 12) ÷ ____ = 8
4 24 + (3 × ____) = 10 × 6
5 (5 × 9) + 4 = 7 × ____
6 88 ÷ ____ = 11 × 2
7 26 – 6 – 2 = 9 × ____
8 6 × 200 = 3 × ____
9 $\frac{1}{2}$ × 26 = ____ + 6
10 240 ÷ 8 = 120 ÷ ____

I wonder if guessing and checking would help?

Score

D Complete.

1 2 × 7 × 3 = 6 × ____
2 $4^2 + 8^2$ = (4 × ____) + (8 × ____)
3 72 – 18 = (8 × ____) – (6 × ____)
4 $\frac{1}{2}$ × 64 = ($\frac{1}{2}$ × ____) + ($\frac{1}{2}$ × 4)
5 (7 × 9) + 9 = ____ × 9
6 6 × 12 = 3 × ____
7 (48 ÷ 4) + ____ = 3 × 7
8 500 × 4 = 250 × ____
9 56 ÷ (____ – 1) = 7
10 360 ÷ 6 = ____ ÷ 3

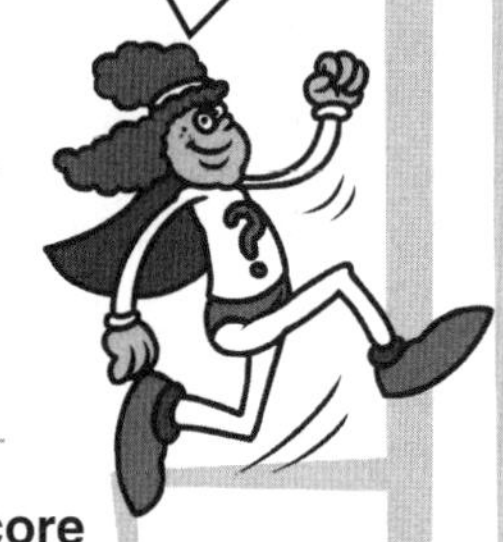

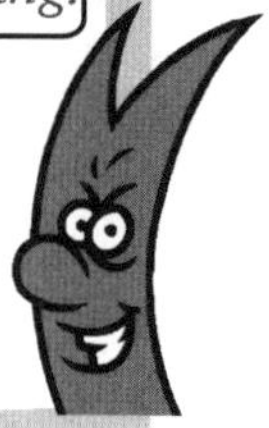

Look for partitioning.

Score

Listen and Write

1 ____ 6 ____
2 ____ 7 ____
3 ____ 8 ____
4 ____ 9 ____
5 ____ 10 ____

Score

Think About It!

Follow the formula to help you finish the grid.

Formula: x = (y – 5) × 3 + 2

x	8							
y	7	10	5	15	8	20	9	12

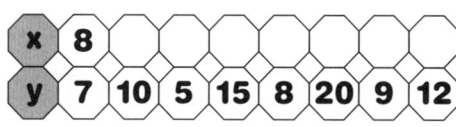

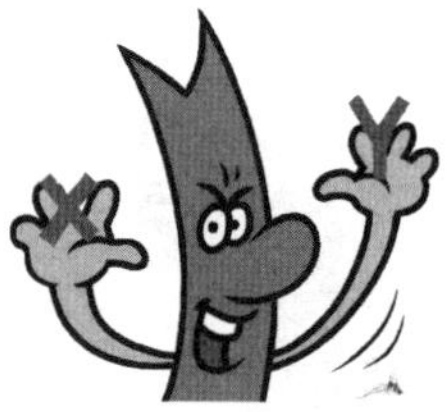

Learning objective

- *Use appropriate number operations to solve problems.*

Review 2

A Complete.
1. 9 × 7 = _____
2. 5 × 9 = _____
3. 56 ÷ 7 = _____
4. 24 ÷ 6 = _____
5. 3 × _____ = 24
6. _____ ÷ 7 = 7
7. _____ × 9 = 54
8. 48 ÷ _____ = 8
9. 4 × 9 = _____
10. 64 ÷ 8 = _____

→ Score

B Complete.
1. Product of 7 and 4? _____
2. Difference between 24 and 9? _____
3. Sum of 8, 6 and 9? _____
4. Share £1.80 among 3 _____
5. 7 @ 55p each = _____
6. Add 6 to the product of 9 and 5 _____
7. $\frac{1}{4}$ of £20 = _____
8. Subtract 9 from the sum of 18 and 7 _____
9. £12.50 = _____ pence
10. £10 − £4.95 = _____

→ Score

C Complete.
1. $\frac{1}{2}$ of 12 = _____
2. $\frac{1}{4}$ × 24 = _____
3. 0.2 as a fraction _____
4. $\frac{1}{4}$ as a decimal _____
5. 1.1 − 0.7 = _____
6. $\frac{1}{5}$ of 40 = _____
7. 7.1 as a fraction _____
8. $\frac{1}{5}$ as a decimal _____
9. $\frac{2}{3}$ × 18 = _____
10. $\frac{3}{5}$ of 35 = _____

→ Score

D Complete.
1. (54 ÷ 6) + 8 = _____
2. (7 × _____) − 5 = 4 × 11
3. 6 × 200 = 3 × _____ = 12 × _____
4. 8 @ £1.50 each = _____
5. $\frac{1}{2}$ of £30 = _____
6. 2.5 + 3.8 = _____
7. $\frac{1}{3}$ + $\frac{1}{6}$ = _____
8. £5 − £1.25 = _____
9. $1\frac{1}{2}$ − $\frac{3}{4}$ = _____
10. $\frac{1}{3}$ × 24 + $\frac{1}{4}$ of 16 = _____

→ Score

Listen and Write
1. _____   6. _____
2. _____   7. _____
3. _____   8. _____
4. _____   9. _____
5. _____   10. _____

→ Score

Think About It!

Use **2 3 4** and **5** only once to complete this number sentence.

☐ × ⬠ + △ − ◯ = 9

Check-up
- I can derive quickly division facts corresponding to multiplication facts to 10 × 10.
- I can find simple fractions of numbers.
- I can recognise equivalence between fractions and decimals.

22

© OUP: Copying permitted for purchasing school only.

Take a Break   2

The SoupaHeroes have just finished their archery contest. Each SoupaHero had 8 turns in which they fired three arrows. Here is the target.

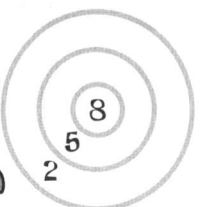

If no SoupaHero missed the target…

1 What was the highest score possible? _____

2 What was the lowest score possible? _____

Here is the scoresheet from the contest.

Round	SoupaGuy			Batboy			WonderGal			Ribbon		
	1	2	3	1	2	3	1	2	3	1	2	3
1	8	8	5	8	2	5	8	8	5			
2	8	5	8	8	5	2	5	8	2			
3	5	5	5	8	8	8	5	5	5	8	8	8
4	8	5	2	5	5	2	5	8	8	8	2	5
5	8	5	2	5	5	2	2	5	5	5	5	8
6	8	8	8	8	5	5	2	5	8	5	5	5
7	8	2	2				8	8	8	2	8	2
8	2	5	2				5	8	5	5	8	2
Total					132						135	

3 What was SoupaGuy's total score? _____

4 Write a set of possible scores for Batboy in his last two rounds of the contest.
Round 7 _____ _____ _____
Round 8 _____ _____ _____

5 What was WonderGal's total score? _____

6 Write a set of possible scores for Ribbon in her first two rounds of the contest.
Round 1 _____ _____ _____
Round 2 _____ _____ _____

7 Who won the contest and what was the winning score? _____

• Choose and use appropriate number operations and ways of calculating to solve problems.

UNIT 11 Number Facts

Strategies
- rearrange, reorder, partition
- check subtraction by adding and addition by subtraction
- check multiplication by dividing and division by multiplying

A Complete.
1. 18 − 9 = _____
2. 8 × 5 = _____
3. 7 + 9 = _____
4. 28 ÷ 4 = _____
5. 5 + 8 = _____
6. 16 − 7 = _____
7. 24 ÷ 3 = _____
8. 42 ÷ 6 = _____
9. 3 × 7 = _____
10. 9 × 4 = _____

→ Score

Remember: when adding positive numbers the answer will be more.

B Complete.
1. 17 − 8 = _____
2. 9 × 5 = _____
3. 6 + 11 = _____
4. 32 ÷ 4 = _____
5. 7 + 6 = _____
6. 15 − 8 = _____
7. 36 ÷ 6 = _____
8. 54 ÷ 9 = _____
9. 4 × 6 = _____
10. 8 × 5 = _____

→ Score

Remember: when subtracting positive numbers the answer will be less.

C Complete.
1. 16 − _____ = 8
2. 7 × _____ = 42
3. 9 × _____ = 63
4. _____ + 9 = 14
5. _____ ÷ 5 = 8
6. _____ − 7 = 9
7. 48 ÷ _____ = 4
8. _____ × 8 = 64
9. _____ × 7 = 28
10. 9 + _____ = 21

→ Score

Remember: multiplication is repeated addition.

D Complete.
1. _____ − 6 = 8
2. _____ × 8 = 48
3. _____ + 6 = 22
4. _____ ÷ 7 = 7
5. 18 ÷ _____ = 6
6. 5 × _____ = 45
7. 8 + _____ = 17
8. 21 − _____ = 9
9. 9 × 9 = _____
10. 72 ÷ 8 = _____

→ Score

Remember: division is repeated subtraction.

Listen and Write
1. _____   6. _____
2. _____   7. _____
3. _____   8. _____
4. _____   9. _____
5. _____   10. _____

→ Score

Think About It!
To solve this puzzle SoupaGuy must use the numbers in the box to make four true equations.

☐ × ☐ = ☐
☐ ÷ ☐ = ☐
☐ + ☐ = ☐

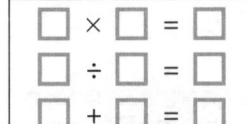

SoupaGuy can use each number once only.

| 2 | 3 | 5 | 7 | 8 |
| 9 | 13 | 18 | 21 | |

Learning objectives
- Know multiplication facts up to 10 × 10 and derive quickly corresponding division facts.
- Derive quickly addition and subtraction facts to 20.

24

© OUP: Copying permitted for purchasing school only.

UNIT 12 Measurement: Time

Strategies
- make all measurements the same units
- speed × time = distance (e.g. 90 km/h for 3 hours = 270 km)
- distance ÷ speed = time (e.g. 270 km @ 90 km/h takes 3 hours)
- distance ÷ time = speed (e.g. 270 km in 3 hours = 90 km/h)

A Complete.
Remember: to change hours to minutes or minutes to seconds multiply by 60.

1. $2\frac{1}{2}$ hours = _____ minutes
2. 20 km/h for 2 hours = _____ km
3. $\frac{1}{4}$ hour = _____ minutes
4. 100 km at 50 km/h = _____ hours
5. $1\frac{1}{2}$ minutes = _____ seconds
6. 11:30 – 5 minutes = _____
7. Days in December? _____
8. 200 km in 4 hours = _____ km/h
9. 3 fortnights = _____ days
10. 1:15 + 25 minutes = _____

→ Score

B Complete.
Remember: to change minutes to hours and minutes divide by 60.

1. $4\frac{1}{2}$ hours = _____ minutes
2. 50 km/h for 10 hours = _____ km
3. $\frac{3}{4}$ hour = _____ minutes
4. 300 km in 3 hours = _____ km/h
5. $3\frac{1}{2}$ minutes = _____ secs
6. 5 minutes before midday? = _____
7. Days in April and May? _____
8. 150 km at 50 km/h = _____ hours
9. 8 decades = _____ years
10. 9:30 + 45 minutes = _____

→ Score

C Complete.
Remember: to change seconds to minutes and seconds divide by 60.

1. $5\frac{1}{4}$ hours = _____ minutes
2. 5 km/h for 4 hours = _____ km
3. $\frac{1}{5}$ hour = _____ minutes
4. 120 km at 20 km/h = _____ hours
5. $2\frac{1}{4}$ minutes = _____ secs
6. 15 minutes before 5:30 a.m. = _____
7. Days in June and July? _____
8. $5\frac{1}{2}$ centuries = _____ years
9. 250 km in 5 hours = _____ km
10. 45 minutes after 11:45 a.m. = _____

→ Score

D Complete.
Remember: to change days to hours multiply by 24.

1. $7\frac{3}{4}$ hours = _____ minutes
2. 25 km/h for 8 hours = _____ km
3. $\frac{1}{12}$ hour = _____ minutes
4. 75 km at 15 km/h = _____ hours
5. $10\frac{1}{2}$ minutes = _____ seconds
6. 7:05 p.m. – 10 minutes = _____
7. Days in August, September, October? _____
8. $6\frac{1}{2}$ years = _____ months
9. 6 km in $1\frac{1}{2}$ hours = _____ km/h
10. 5:20 a.m. + 55 minutes = _____

→ Score

Listen and Write

1. _____   6. _____
2. _____   7. _____
3. _____   8. _____
4. _____   9. _____
5. _____   10. _____

→ Score

Think About It!
How many…?

a. minutes in half a day? _____
b. days in 12 weeks? _____
c. fortnights in 3 months? _____
d. months in 8 years? _____

Learning objectives
- Convert larger to smaller units of time and vice versa.
- Use units of time to solve simple problems involving time.

25

© OUP: Copying permitted for purchasing school only.

UNIT 13 Fractions and Decimals

Strategies
- before adding or subtracting, find equivalent fractions by multiplying or dividing the denominators
- common fraction × whole number = numerator × whole number ÷ denominator

A Complete.

1. $\frac{1}{8} + \frac{3}{8} =$ _____
2. $\frac{5}{6} - \frac{4}{6} =$ _____
3. $\frac{1}{2}$ of 24 = _____
4. $\frac{1}{4}$ of 12 = _____
5. As a decimal? $\frac{1}{2} =$ _____
6. As a fraction? 0.4 = _____
7. 0.6 + 0.5 = _____
8. 0.8 − 0.5 = _____
9. $\frac{1}{2}$ of 5 = _____
10. $\frac{2}{3}$ of 15 = _____

→ Score

Remember: the number to the left of the decimal point is a whole number.

B Complete.

1. $\frac{1}{5} + \frac{1}{5} + \frac{1}{5} =$ _____
2. $\frac{7}{8} - \frac{3}{8} =$ _____
3. $\frac{1}{4}$ of 16 = _____
4. $\frac{1}{3}$ of 18 = _____
5. As a decimal? $\frac{3}{10} =$ _____
6. As a fraction? 0.5 = _____
7. 0.7 + 0.8 = _____
8. 0.9 − 0.4 = _____
9. 6 × 0.7 = _____
10. $\frac{3}{4}$ of 36 = _____

→ Score

Remember: the number to the right of the decimal point is a fractional number.

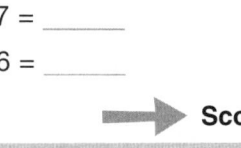

C Complete.

1. $\frac{4}{6} + \frac{1}{6} =$ _____
2. $\frac{3}{5} - \frac{1}{5} =$ _____
3. $\frac{1}{8}$ of 32 = _____
4. $\frac{1}{6}$ of 48 = _____
5. As a decimal? $3\frac{1}{4} =$ _____
6. As a fraction? 1.75 = _____
7. 1.2 + 5.9 = _____
8. 1.1 − 0.6 = _____
9. $\frac{9}{10}$ of 20 = _____
10. $\frac{5}{6}$ of 30 = _____

→ Score

Remember: add digits that hold the same position.

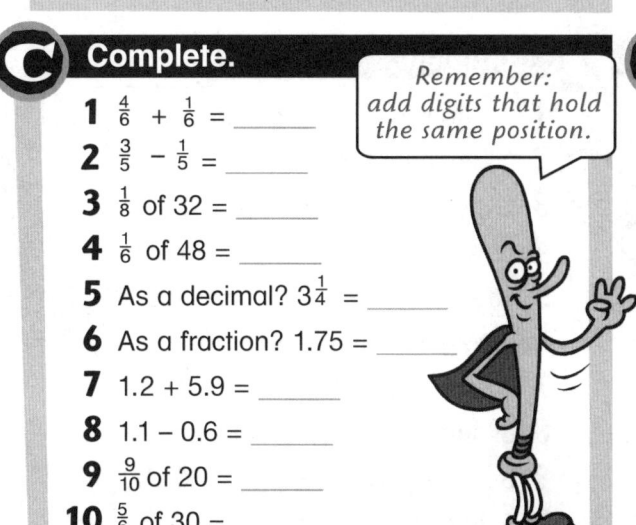

D Complete.

1. $\frac{1}{5} + \frac{1}{10} =$ _____
2. $\frac{1}{4} - \frac{1}{8} =$ _____
3. $\frac{1}{7}$ of 21 = _____
4. $\frac{1}{8}$ of 56 = _____
5. As a decimal? $5\frac{1}{2} =$ _____
6. As a fraction? 6.25 = _____
7. 4.5 + 4.5 + 4.5 = _____
8. 2.3 − 0.8 = _____
9. 7 × 1.2 = _____
10. $\frac{7}{8}$ of 32 = _____

→ Score

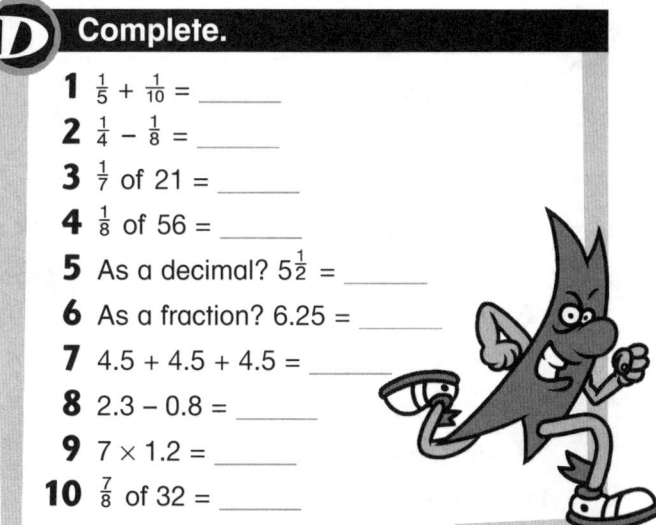

Listen and Write

1. _____   6. _____
2. _____   7. _____
3. _____   8. _____
4. _____   9. _____
5. _____   10. _____

→ Score

Think About It!

The MIGHTY EQUIVALENTS have washed their footy jumpers and hung them up to dry. Unfortunately all of the numbers except one have fallen off.

Write some possible numbers on the jumpers.

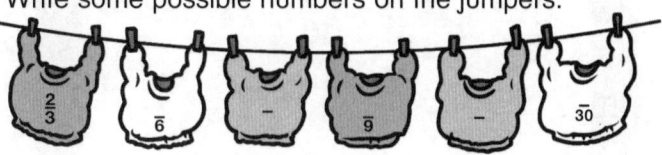

Learning objectives
- Use fraction notation including mixed numbers.
- Relate fractions to their decimal representations.
- Relate fractions to division and use division to find simple fractions.

UNIT 14 Place Value

Strategies
- visualise the Place Value chart
- the value of a digit is determined by the place it occupies

millions			thousands			units		
h	t	u	h	t	u	h	t	u

Remember: zero when used with other numerals changes their value 1(0) = 10.

A Complete.
1. 80 + 70000 + 6000 + 400 + 2 = _____
2. 60 + 400 + 90 000 + 8 = _____
3. 7623 = _____ hundreds + 23 units
4. 8.4 = 8 units + _____ tenths
5. Value of 3 in 234 568? _____
6. 256.8 = 25 tens 6 units _____ tenths
7. 6943 = _____ tens + 3 units
8. 86 234 = _____ thousands + 234 units
9. Value of 5 in 24.5? _____
10. 1000 + 10 000 + 1 = _____

→ Score

B Complete.
1. 1000 more than 6894 = _____
2. Value of 5 in 53 684? _____
3. 500 + 50 000 + 7000 + 80 + 2 = _____
4. 10 000 more than 33 761 = _____
5. Value of 8 in 28.07? _____
6. 784.25 = 700 + 80 + 4 + _____
7. 50 000 + 3000 + 20 000 + 900 + 40 + 1 = _____
8. Value of 6 in 543.67? _____
9. Value of 36 in 89 365? _____
10. 80 + 2 tenths + 6 = _____

→ Score

C Complete.
1. 1000 less than 186 423 _____
2. Value of 8 in 19.08? _____
3. 60 + 400 000 + 7000 + 80 000 + 9 = _____
4. 10 000 more than 578 264 = _____
5. Value of 73 in 173 504? _____
6. $\frac{3}{10}$ + 5 + 90 + $\frac{7}{100}$ = _____
7. 5 000 000 + 800 000 + 900 + 60 000 = _____
8. Value of 26 in 3.26? _____
9. Hundreds in 5000? _____
10. Value of 7 in 879 305? _____

→ Score

D Complete.
1. 100 000 more than 2 536 005? _____
2. Value of 57 in 257 654? _____
3. 30 000 more than 864 529 = _____
4. $\frac{1}{10}$ + 100 000 + $\frac{1}{100}$ + 5000 = _____
5. Value of 16 in 5982.16? _____
6. 1 million less than 7 659 278 = _____
7. 500 000 + 9 + 60 000 + 7000 + 250 + $\frac{18}{100}$ = _____
8. Value of 4 in 7 693 422? _____
9. Value of 5 in 3.5 million? _____
10. Value of 17 in 17 860 294? _____

→ Score

Listen and Write
1. _____ 6. _____
2. _____ 7. _____
3. _____ 8. _____
4. _____ 9. _____
5. _____ 10. _____

→ Score

Think About It!

Write these population figures in full and then the countries in order of population size: largest to smallest (e.g. 8.3 = 8 300 000).

Australia 18$\frac{1}{2}$ million _____
Algeria 26.346 million _____
China 1188 million _____
Egypt 55.2 million _____
Israel 5 million _____
Republic of Seychelles 76 thousand _____

Learning objectives
- Read and write whole numbers in figures and words, and know what each digit represents.
- Know what each digit represents in a number with up to two decimal places.

© OUP: Copying permitted for purchasing school only.

UNIT 15 Doubling and Halving

Strategies
- to double: multiply by 2
- to halve: divide by 2
- break the number down – partition
  (e.g. double 87 = 80 × 2 + 7 × 2; half of 294 = 200 ÷ 2 + 90 ÷ 2 + 4 ÷ 2)

A Complete.

1. 2 × 210 = _____
2. Double 54 = _____
3. 2 × 63 = _____
4. 82 × 2 = _____
5. Double 115 = _____
6. Half of 250 = _____
7. 630 ÷ 2 = _____
8. $\frac{1}{2}$ of 460 = _____
9. Half of 72 = _____
10. $\frac{1}{2}$ × 580 = _____

Remember: double = × 2.

Score

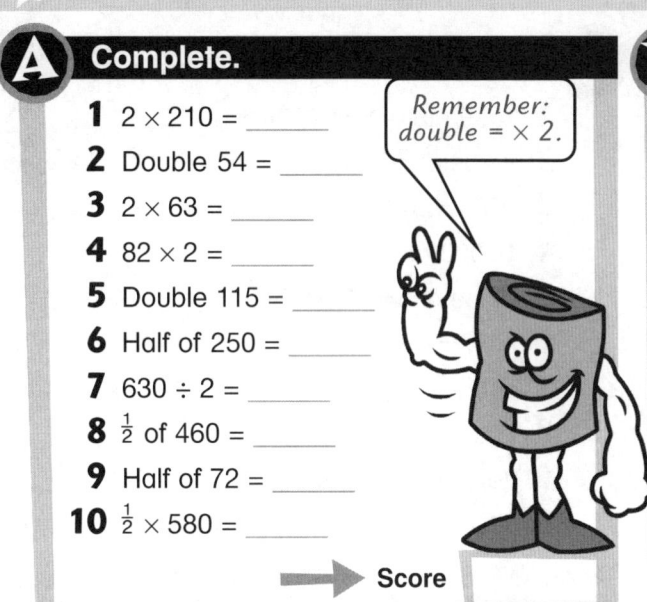

B Complete.

1. $\frac{1}{2}$ of 120 = _____
2. Double 56 = _____
3. 93 × 2 = _____
4. $\frac{1}{2}$ of 604 = _____
5. 59 × 2 = _____
6. Half of 230 = _____
7. Double 136 = _____
8. Half of 162 = _____
9. 148 ÷ 2 = _____
10. 334 × 2 = _____

Remember: halve = ÷ 2.

Score

C Complete.

1. Double 480 = _____
2. 2 × 950 = _____
3. 670 × 2 = _____
4. Double 757 = _____
5. Double 391 = _____
6. Half of 490 = _____
7. Half of 352 = _____
8. $\frac{1}{2}$ of 908 = _____
9. $\frac{1}{2}$ × 1240 = _____
10. $\frac{1}{2}$ of 1806 = _____

Score

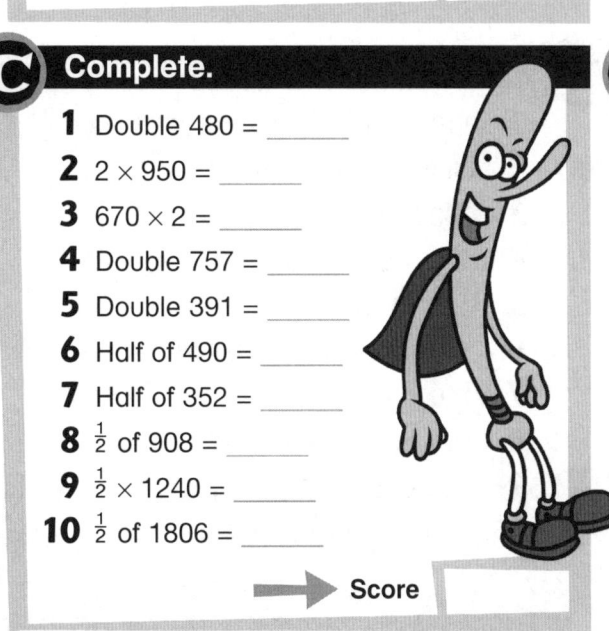

D Complete.

1. Half of 326 = _____
2. Half of 914 = _____
3. Double 737 = _____
4. Double 959 = _____
5. $\frac{1}{2}$ × 1252 = _____
6. $\frac{1}{2}$ of 1648 = _____
7. 595 × 2 = _____
8. 2 × 6073 = _____
9. Double 84.5 = _____
10. Half of 96.8 = _____

Score

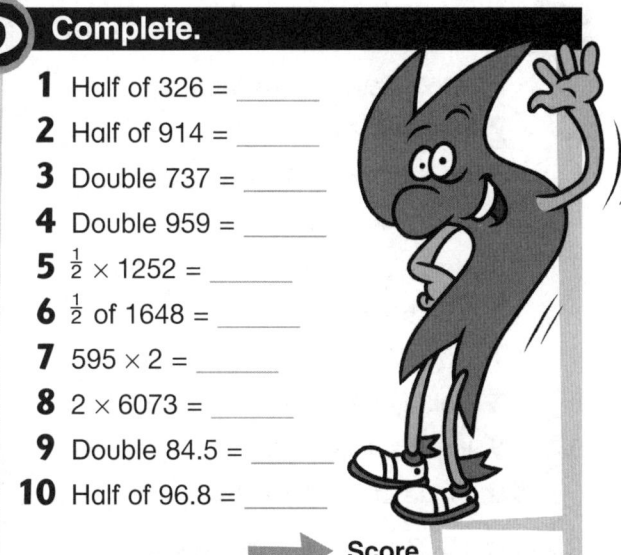

Listen and Write

1. _____   6. _____
2. _____   7. _____
3. _____   8. _____
4. _____   9. _____
5. _____   10. _____

Score

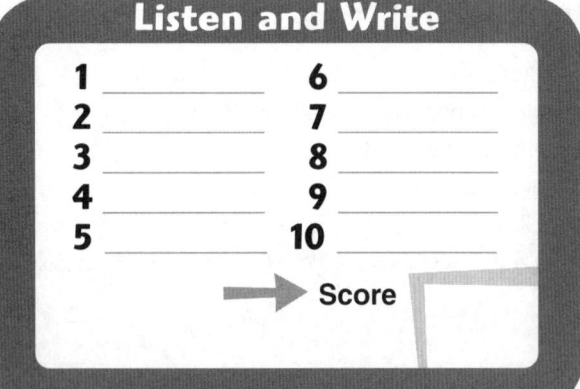

Think About It!

A plant begins its growing season 10 cm tall with 19 leaves.

If it doubles the number of leaves for every 10 centimetres it grows and it is now 50 cm tall, how many leaves does it now have?

_____

Learning objectives
- Derive quickly doubles of whole numbers 1–100, multiples of 10 to 1000, multiples of 100 to 10 000 and corresponding halves.
- Use doubling and halving starting from known facts.

Review 3

A Complete.
1. 17 − 8 = _____
2. 6 + 9 + 4 = _____
3. 9 × 6 = _____
4. 42 ÷ 7 = _____
5. 1:30 + 15 minutes = _____
6. $\frac{7}{8} - \frac{3}{8}$ = _____
7. 250 km in 5 hours = _____ km/h
8. Value of 6 in 564 079? _____
9. Double 765 = _____
10. 0.6 + 0.7 = _____

→ Score

B Complete.
1. 8 + 7 + 6 = _____
2. 7 × 8 = _____
3. 72 ÷ 8 = _____
4. 15 − 8 = _____
5. 9:15 + 15 minutes = _____
6. $\frac{1}{5} + \frac{3}{5} + \frac{4}{5}$ = _____
7. 600 km @ 60 km/h = _____ hours
8. $\frac{3}{10}$ + 2 + 600 + 50 + $\frac{7}{100}$ = _____
9. Half of 926 = _____
10. 1.2 − 0.8 = _____

→ Score

C Complete.
1. 48 ÷ 6 = _____
2. 7 + 6 + 9 = _____
3. 6 × 8 = _____
4. 21 − 8 = _____
5. 7:25 + 15 minutes = _____
6. $\frac{3}{4}$ of 16 = _____
7. 525 km in 5 hours = _____ km/h
8. 10 000 less than 864 927 = _____
9. 532 × 2 = _____
10. 5 × 0.6 = _____

→ Score

D Complete.
1. 9 × 7 = _____
2. 54 ÷ 6 = _____
3. 23 − 9 = _____
4. 8 + 9 + 7 = _____
5. 3:05 + 45 minutes = _____
6. $\frac{5}{8}$ of 40 = _____
7. 120 km in $1\frac{1}{2}$ hours = _____ km/h
8. Value of 35 in 763 502? _____
9. $\frac{1}{2}$ of 572 = _____
10. 8 × 2.3 = _____

→ Score

Listen and Write
1. _____   6. _____
2. _____   7. _____
3. _____   8. _____
4. _____   9. _____
5. _____   10. _____

→ Score

Think About It!

Write the numbers 13 to 20 in the outer squares so that each line totals 42.

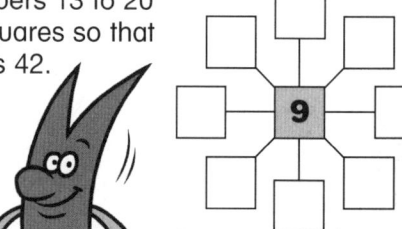

 Check-up
- I can find doubles and halves of 3-digit numbers.
- I can solve simple addition problems involving time.
- I can solve simple problems involving speed and distance.

29

© OUP: Copying permitted for purchasing school only.

Take a Break

3

Back to Work or Working Backwards

How quickly can you work out the number each SoupaHero is hiding on the reverse of the cards?

If you halve my number and then add 9, you get 14.

If you double my number and then add 8, you get 20.

If you multiply my number by 3 then divide by 4, you get 6.

If you subtract 3 from my number then multiply by 4 and halve the result, you get 18.

Learning objective: Choose and use appropriate number operations to solve problems.

UNIT 16 Number Facts

Strategies
- visualise (e.g. 6 × 3 = 6 groups of 3, 24 ÷ 4 = 24 shared among 4)
- rearrange to simplify (e.g. 72 ÷ 8 = ? so 8 × ? = 72)

A Complete.
Remember: A × B = B × A.

1. 5 × 6 = _____
2. _____ × 7 = 63
3. _____ ÷ 8 = 5
4. 7 × 8 = _____
5. 24 ÷ 3 = _____
6. 72 ÷ _____ = 9
7. 9 × 4 = _____
8. 36 ÷ 6 = _____
9. 9 × 0 = _____
10. _____ × 8 = 64

Score

B Complete.
Remember: A ÷ B = C is the same as C × B = A.

1. 7 × 9 = _____
2. 5 × _____ = 45
3. 16 ÷ 8 = _____
4. 66 ÷ 6 = _____
5. 8 × 4 = _____
6. 81 ÷ 9 = _____
7. _____ × 8 = 0
8. 80 ÷ _____ = 10
9. _____ ÷ 6 = 9
10. 7 × 7 = _____

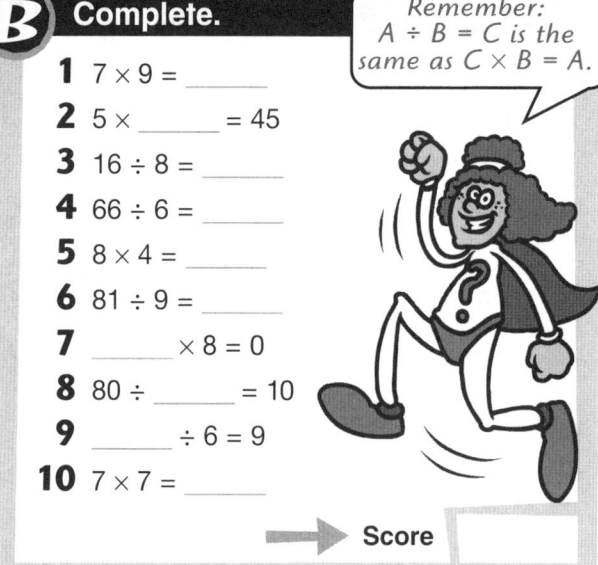

Score

C Complete.
Remember: A + B + C = A + C + B = B + A + C.

1. 4 × 7 = _____
2. 6 × 7 = _____
3. 12 ÷ 3 = _____
4. 27 ÷ 9 = _____
5. _____ × 8 = 24
6. _____ × 6 = 42
7. 15 ÷ _____ = 5
8. 48 ÷ 6 = _____
9. 18 ÷ 9 = _____
10. 9 × 3 = _____

Score

D Complete.
Remember: A − B = C is the same as C + B = A.

1. 48 ÷ 4 = _____
2. 6 × 6 = _____
3. 54 ÷ 9 = _____
4. 4^2 = _____
5. 8 × 8 = _____
6. 24 ÷ 12 = _____
7. 63 ÷ 7 = _____
8. 7^2 = _____
9. 8 × 7 = _____
10. 12 × 9 = _____

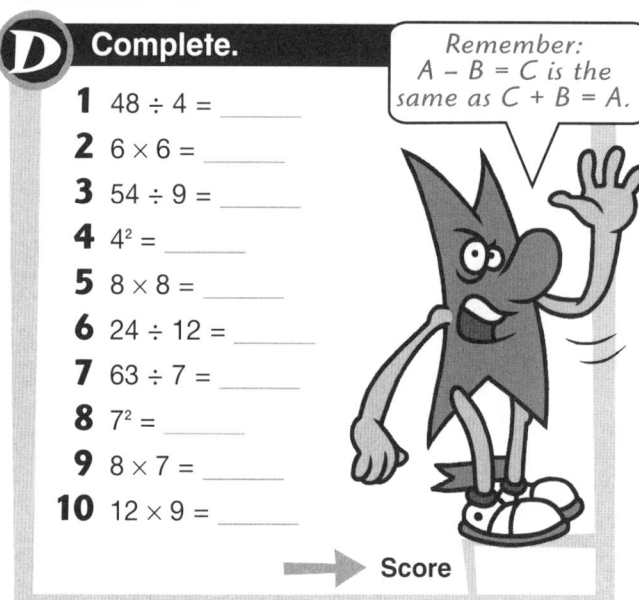

Score

Listen and Write

1. _____   6. _____
2. _____   7. _____
3. _____   8. _____
4. _____   9. _____
5. _____   10. _____

Score

Think About It!

Use the numbers **3 4 9** and **12** to make the following number sentence true.

There may be more than one solution.

Learning objective
- Know by heart multiplication facts up to 10 × 10 and derive quickly corresponding division facts.

UNIT 17 Equations

Strategies
- carry out the operations one stage at a time
- use order of operations ( ) of × ÷ + −
- one side of = must be of the same value as the other side

A Complete.
Remember: ( ) first...

1. $(6 - 2) \times (4 + 4) = $ _____
2. (_____ $\times 8) + (2 \times 8) = 96$
3. $(8 \times 3) + (\frac{1}{4}$ of $16) = $ _____
4. $(9 \times 7) - (6 \times 8) = $ _____
5. $(10 \times 9) - (5 \times 9) = $ _____ $\times 9$
6. $10 \times 10 \times 30 = $ _____
7. $(£50 - £16) + (£50 - £24) = $ _____
8. $10 \times $ _____ $= 8 \times 5$
9. $\frac{1}{4}$ of $24 = 6 \times $ _____
10. $(\frac{1}{10}$ of $100) - (\frac{1}{3} \times 15) = $ _____

➡ Score ____

B Complete.
Remember: ... then of...

1. $(9 \div 3) \times (12 \div 4) = $ _____
2. $(5 \times 6) + ($ _____ $\times 6) = $ _____ $\times 6 = 90$
3. $(24 \div 3) + (\frac{3}{4} \times 12) = $ _____
4. $5 \times 5 \times 5 + 100 = $ _____ $+ 100 = $ _____
5. $12 \times $ _____ $= 6 \times 20 = $ _____
6. $(\frac{1}{4}$ of $100) - (\frac{1}{5}$ of $20) = $ _____
7. $(£10 - £3) + (£10 - £7) + (£10 - £5) = $ _____
8. $(\frac{1}{3}$ of $27) \times (\frac{1}{5}$ of $40) = $ _____
9. $(10 + 20) \times 5 = $ _____
10. $(9 + 8) - (36 \div 6) = $ _____

➡ Score ____

C Complete.
Remember: ... then × or ÷...

1. $(7 + 5) \times (\frac{1}{4}$ of $24) = $ _____
2. $(£20 - £12) + (£20 - £11) = $ _____
3. $(10 \times 6) + (10 \times 6) + (7 \times 6) = $ _____ $\times 6$
4. $(\frac{1}{3}$ of $15) \times (\frac{1}{8}$ of $32) = $ _____
5. $(8 \times 7) - (6 \times 6) = $ _____
6. $24 \times $ _____ $= 48 \times 5$
7. $(54 \div 9) + (18 \div 3) = $ _____
8. $(3 \times 10) + ($__$\times 10) + ($__$\times 4) = (3 \times $__$) = 72$
9. $(\frac{1}{4}$ of $24) \times (\frac{1}{5}$ of $40) = $ _____
10. $5 \times 4 \times 3 = $ _____

➡ Score ____

D Complete.
Remember: ... finally + or −.

1. $\frac{1}{4}$ of $(12 \times 10) = $ _____
2. $\frac{1}{4}$ of $12 \times 10 = $ _____
3. $(£10 - £6) \times (20 - 12) = $ _____
4. $(\frac{3}{4}$ of $20) \times (\frac{1}{5}$ of $20) = $ _____
5. $18 \times 5 = 9 \times $ _____
6. $(7 \times 4) + (7 \times 4) + (7 \times 4) + (7 \times 4) = $ _____ $\times 4$
7. $(60 \div 6) \times (35 \div 7) = $ _____
8. $(10 \times 8) + (7 \times 8) = $ _____ $\times 8$
9. $(36 \div 9) \times (24 \div 8) = $ _____
10. $(12 \div 3) \times (7 - 6) = $ _____

➡ Score ____

Listen and Write

1 ____ 6 ____
2 ____ 7 ____
3 ____ 8 ____
4 ____ 9 ____
5 ____ 10 ____

➡ Score ____

Think About It!

SoupaGuy is making footwarmers for his pets. Rather than count all the feet, he wants to write a number sentence to make things quicker. SoupaGuy has 9 dogs, 7 cats and 6 budgies. Write the number sentence that SoupaGuy might use and the number of footwarmers that he will need to make.

_____

Learning objective
- Choose and use appropriate number operations and ways of calculating to solve number problems.

UNIT 18 Measurement: Mass

Strategies
- use knowledge of basic number facts
- change to common units
- ask, 'Will the answer be more or less?'
- estimate your answer
- learn and use measurement tables

A Complete.

Remember: 1000 g = 1 kg.

1. 450 g + 260 g = _____
2. 1.5 kg + 1.5 kg = _____
3. 7 kg × 9 = _____
4. 500 g × 6 = _____
5. 5.4 kg + 300 g = _____
6. 9 kg − 500 g = _____
7. 500 g @ £12 per kg = _____
8. 2500 g = _____ kg
9. 1.2 kg = _____ g
10. 500 g ÷ 10 = _____

→ Score

B Complete.

Remember: when multiplying by 10, shift the digits 1 place left.

1. 8.2 kg − 300 g = _____
2. 1.7 kg + 900 g = _____
3. 5.5 kg × 3 = _____
4. 2000 g ÷ 5 = _____
5. 250 g × 10 = _____
6. 3.9 kg + 700 g = _____
7. 250 g @ £24 per kg = _____
8. 1.5 kg ÷ 3 = _____ g
9. 750 g × 3 = _____ kg
10. 5.3 kg = _____ g

→ Score

C Complete.

Remember: when dividing by 10, shift the decimal point 1 place to the left.

1. 3.5 kg + 850 g = _____
2. 7.2 kg − 600 g = _____
3. 2.5 kg × 8 = _____
4. 5.6 kg ÷ 7 = _____
5. 320 g × 10 = _____
6. 80p a kilo. How much for 1½ kg? _____
7. 500 g @ £1.50 per kg = _____
8. 1.5 tonne = _____ kg
9. ½ of 2.8 kg = _____
10. 87.5 kg ÷ 10 = _____

→ Score

D Complete.

Remember: 1000 kg = 1 tonne.

1. 5.2 kg + 0.7 kg + 250 g = _____
2. 6.5 kg − 900 g = _____
3. 24.6 kg ÷ 3 = _____
4. 430 g × 5 = _____
5. 75.5 kg × 10 = _____
6. £1.60 a kilo. How much for 250 g? _____
7. 250 g @ £4.80 per kg = _____
8. 10.5 tonnes = _____ kg
9. ¼ × 3.6 kg = _____
10. 2.25 kg ÷ 10 = _____

→ Score

Listen and Write

1. _____ 6. _____
2. _____ 7. _____
3. _____ 8. _____
4. _____ 9. _____
5. _____ 10. _____

→ Score

Think About It!

On a set of scales, a housebrick balances with three 250 g weights and half a housebrick.

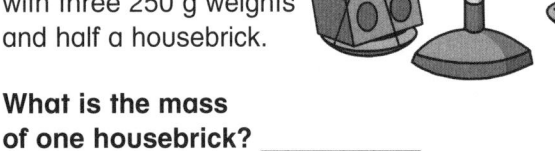

What is the mass of one housebrick? _____

Learning objectives
- Convert larger to smaller units.
- Solve problems involving measures (mass).

UNIT 19 Percentages

Strategies
- how many out of 100?
- make the denominator 100
- reduce fractions to lowest terms

A Write as percentages.
1. $\frac{50}{100}$ = _____
2. $\frac{20}{100}$ = _____
3. $\frac{10}{100}$ = _____
4. $\frac{30}{100}$ = _____
5. $\frac{90}{100}$ = _____
6. $\frac{25}{100}$ = _____
7. $\frac{75}{100}$ = _____
8. $\frac{15}{100}$ = _____
9. $\frac{83}{100}$ = _____
10. $\frac{1}{100}$ = _____

Score ____

B Write as fractions.
1. 75% = _____
2. 10% = _____
3. 25% = _____
4. 100% = _____
5. 22% = _____
6. 56% = _____
7. 8% = _____
8. 94% = _____
9. 17% = _____
10. 33% = _____

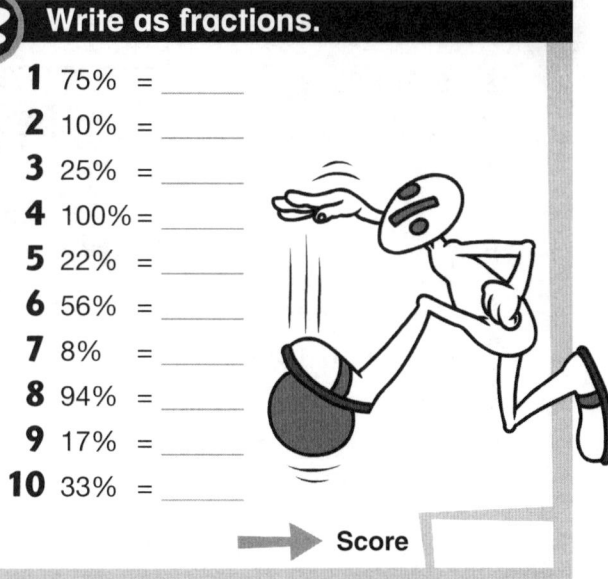

Score ____

C Write as percentages.
1. $\frac{25}{50}$ = _____
2. $\frac{10}{50}$ = _____
3. $\frac{30}{50}$ = _____
4. $\frac{5}{50}$ = _____
5. $\frac{40}{50}$ = _____
6. $\frac{15}{50}$ = _____
7. $\frac{30}{50}$ = _____
8. $\frac{20}{25}$ = _____
9. $\frac{12}{25}$ = _____
10. $\frac{16}{25}$ = _____

Score ____

D Write as percentages.
1. $\frac{1}{2}$ = _____
2. $\frac{1}{10}$ = _____
3. $\frac{1}{4}$ = _____
4. $\frac{1}{20}$ = _____
5. $\frac{3}{4}$ = _____
6. $\frac{3}{10}$ = _____
7. $\frac{1}{5}$ = _____
8. $\frac{1}{25}$ = _____
9. $\frac{7}{10}$ = _____
10. $\frac{2}{5}$ = _____

Score ____

Listen and Write
1. ____   6. ____
2. ____   7. ____
3. ____   8. ____
4. ____   9. ____
5. ____   10. ____

Score ____

Think About It!

During the game...
- Ace scored 3 times from 6 shots.
- Bomber scored once from 10 shots.
- Masher scored 3 out of 4 shots.
- Whoosh scored 5 times and had 20 shots.
- Slammer scored 4 times from 5 shots.

Who shot the best goal percentage? ____

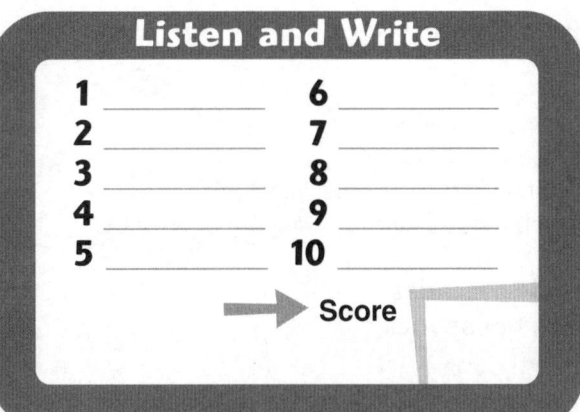

Learning objective
- Express one half, one quarter, three quarters and tenths and hundredths as percentages.

34

© OUP: Copying permitted for purchasing school only.

UNIT 20 Counting and Order

Strategies
- ask, 'Am I counting forwards or backwards?'
- ask, 'What am I counting by?'
- ask, 'Is there more than one operation?'
- look for digits or groups of digits that repeat
- use place value to order numbers

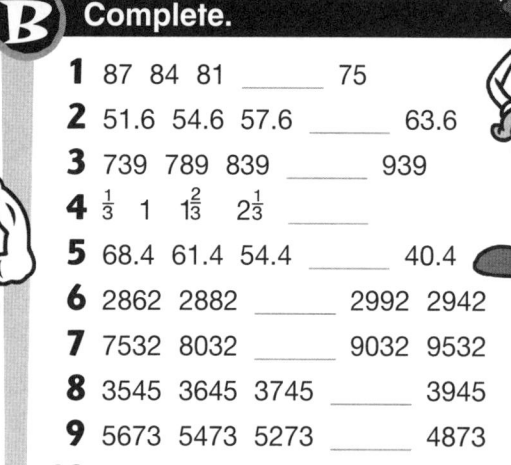

Remember: when counting forwards the numbers get larger.

Remember: when counting backwards the numbers get smaller.

A Complete.
1. 62 67 ___ 77 82
2. 54 50 46 ___ 38
3. 629 619 609 ___ 589
4. 24.1 24.3 24.5 ___ 24.9
5. $\frac{1}{4}$ $\frac{2}{4}$ $\frac{3}{4}$ ___ $1\frac{1}{4}$
6. 284 293 ___ 311 320
7. 765.3 760.3 755.3 ___ 745.3
8. 363 333 303 273 ___
9. $1\frac{4}{8}$ $1\frac{3}{8}$ $1\frac{2}{8}$ $1\frac{1}{8}$ ___
10. 246 276 306 336 ___

→ Score

B Complete.
1. 87 84 81 ___ 75
2. 51.6 54.6 57.6 ___ 63.6
3. 739 789 839 ___ 939
4. $\frac{1}{3}$ 1 $1\frac{2}{3}$ $2\frac{1}{3}$ ___
5. 68.4 61.4 54.4 ___ 40.4
6. 2862 2882 ___ 2992 2942
7. 7532 8032 ___ 9032 9532
8. 3545 3645 3745 ___ 3945
9. 5673 5473 5273 ___ 4873
10. 9213 8213 7213 ___ 5213

→ Score

C Complete.
1. 329 331 333 335 ___
2. 5284 6284 7284 ___ 9284
3. 1.25 1.5 1.75 2 ___
4. $\frac{1}{6}$ $\frac{1}{2}$ $\frac{5}{6}$ $1\frac{1}{6}$ ___
5. 976 946 916 ___ 856
6. 7234 9234 11234 ___ 15234
7. 145 545 945 ___ 1745
8. 35.1 32.1 29.1 26.1 ___
9. 220 310 400 ___ 580
10. 50.4 50.7 51 51.3 ___

→ Score

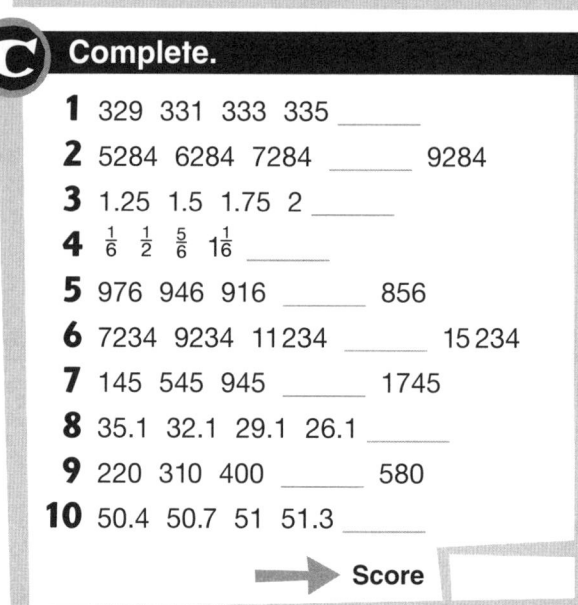

D Complete.
1. 7345 7545 7745 ___ 8145
2. 28.6 39.6 ___ 61.6 72.6
3. $\frac{1}{8}$ $\frac{1}{2}$ $\frac{7}{8}$ $1\frac{1}{4}$ ___
4. 6768 6468 6168 ___ 5568
5. 9625 13625 ___ 21625 25625
6. 413.1 416.1 ___ 422.1 425.1
7. 64 128 256 ___ 1024
8. 8533 7833 7133 ___ 5733
9. 896 448 224 112 ___
10. 12.75 17.75 ___ 27.75 32.75

→ Score

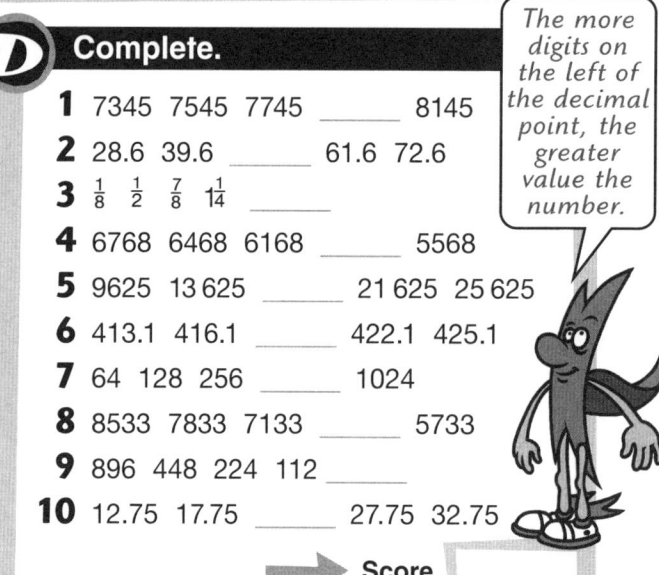

The more digits on the left of the decimal point, the greater value the number.

Listen and Write
1. ___   6. ___
2. ___   7. ___
3. ___   8. ___
4. ___   9. ___
5. ___   10. ___

→ Score

Think About It!

Write in order: smallest to largest.

a 2020   2.02   20.2   2202   20.22

b 15   0.5   150   15.5   1.5   0.15

Learning objective
- Recognise and extend number sequences.

35

Review 4

A Complete.

1. 9 × 7 = _____
2. 7 × 4 = _____
3. Value of 5 in 275.83? _____
4. £72 ÷ 8 = _____
5. $3\frac{1}{2}$ hours = _____ minutes
6. Double 79 = _____
7. 500 g @ £14 per kilo = _____
8. Next? 684 724 764 804 _____
9. $\frac{1}{4}$ of 24 = _____
10. 6 × 0.5 = _____

➔ Score _____

B Complete.

1. 6 × 7 = _____
2. As a percentage? $\frac{20}{100}$ _____
3. 7 × 0.4 = _____
4. (70 ÷ 10) × 3 = _____
5. $\frac{1}{3}$ of 36 = _____
6. 250 g @ £12 per kilo = _____
7. Next? 8 16 32 64 _____
8. 55 minutes after 1:15 p.m. = _____
9. Half of 592 = _____
10. 54 kg ÷ 6 = _____

➔ Score _____

C Complete.

1. 9 × 9 = _____
2. As a fraction? 50% = _____
3. 250 g @ £2.40 per kilo = _____
4. (6 × 5) + (10 × 5) = _____ × 5 = _____
5. Next? 22.3 17.3 12.3 7.3 _____
6. $\frac{2}{5}$ of 20 = _____
7. (54 ÷ 6) − ($\frac{1}{3}$ of 9) = _____
8. $9\frac{1}{2}$ minutes = _____ seconds
9. Double 427 = _____
10. 3.2 × 3 = _____

➔ Score _____

D Complete.

1. 8 × 8 = _____
2. As a percentage? $\frac{1}{10}$ = _____
3. Value of 4 in 19.47? _____
4. 60 km/h for $2\frac{1}{2}$ hours = _____ km
5. 7 × 2.3 = _____
6. As a fraction? 25% = _____
7. 750 g @ £20 per kilo = _____
8. Next? 8741 8441 8141 7841 _____
9. $\frac{3}{4}$ of 36 = _____
10. 250 g × 10 = _____

➔ Score _____

Listen and Write

1. _____   6. _____
2. _____   7. _____
3. _____   8. _____
4. _____   9. _____
5. _____   10. _____

➔ Score _____

Think About It!

- A length of ribbon is cut in half and one half is used.
- One third of the remaining piece of ribbon is cut off and used.

If the ribbon that is left is 6 cm long, how long was the ribbon to start with? _____

- I can multiply 1-place decimals by a single-digit number.
- I know and can use the relationships between units of time.
- I can write simple fractions and percentages and vice versa.

Take a Break

4

How quickly can you complete Eratosthenes' Sieve?

Like the ancient Greek mathematician Eratosthenes, you can find all of the prime numbers between 1 and 100 by following instructions.

On the 10 × 10 grid below:

1 Colour number 1.

2 Colour all even numbers except 2.

3 Colour all multiples of 3 except 3.

4 Colour all multiples of 5 except 5.

5 Colour all multiples of 7 except 7.

6 Circle all of the numbers that remain: these are prime numbers.

How many prime numbers are there between 1 and 100? _____

1	2	3	4	5	6	7	8	9	10
11	12	13	14	15	16	17	18	19	20
21	22	23	24	25	26	27	28	29	30
31	32	33	34	35	36	37	38	39	40
41	42	43	44	45	46	47	48	49	50
51	52	53	54	55	56	57	58	59	60
61	62	63	64	65	66	67	68	69	70
71	72	73	74	75	76	77	78	79	80
81	82	83	84	85	86	87	88	89	90
91	92	93	94	95	96	97	98	99	100

Learning objective

- Recognise multiples (of single-digit numbers) up to the 10th multiple.

UNIT 21 Number Facts

Strategies
- visualise grouping for × (multiplication)
- visualise sharing for ÷ (division)
- rearrange, reorder, partition
- check by working backwards

A Complete.

Remember: 4^2 is 4 squared...

1. $7 \times 5 = \underline{}$
2. $\underline{} \times 4 = 24$
3. $20 \div 5 = \underline{}$
4. $15 \div \underline{} = 3$
5. $7 + 6 = \underline{}$
6. $11 - 5 = \underline{}$
7. $7 \times 0 = \underline{}$
8. $80 \div \underline{} = 8$
9. $7^2 = \underline{}$
10. $6 \times 6 = \underline{}$

Score

B Complete.

Remember: ... which means 4×4.

1. $8 \times 4 = \underline{}$
2. $\underline{} \times 9 = 27$
3. $33 \div 3 = \underline{}$
4. $42 \div 7 = \underline{}$
5. $8 + 9 = \underline{}$
6. $16 - 8 = \underline{}$
7. $24 \div \underline{} = 3$
8. $9 + \underline{} = 16$
9. $0 \times 9 = \underline{}$
10. $5^2 = \underline{}$

Score

C Complete.

Remember: if $6 \times 4 = 24$ then $24 \div 4 = 6$ and $24 \div 6 = 4$.

1. $9 \times 6 = \underline{}$
2. $\underline{} \times 8 = 16$
3. $48 \div 6 = \underline{}$
4. $50 \div \underline{} = 10$
5. $4 + 7 = \underline{}$
6. $15 - 9 = \underline{}$
7. $8^2 = \underline{}$
8. $8 \times 0 = \underline{}$
9. $\underline{} \div 5 = 7$
10. $18 - \underline{} = 9$

Score

D Complete.

Remember: if $8 + 6 = 14$ then $14 - 6 = 8$ and $14 - 8 = 6$.

1. $7 \times 8 = \underline{}$
2. $\underline{} \times 5 = 45$
3. $72 \div 8 = \underline{}$
4. $64 \div \underline{} = 8$
5. $9 + 6 = \underline{}$
6. $12 - 7 = \underline{}$
7. $\underline{} \div 4 = 6$
8. $\underline{} \times 8 = 40$
9. $5 \times \underline{} = 0$
10. $9^2 = \underline{}$

Score

Listen and Write

1. _____   6. _____
2. _____   7. _____
3. _____   8. _____
4. _____   9. _____
5. _____   10. _____

Score

Think About It!

Under 1 minute means you're a champ!

QUICK GRID: Time yourself.

×	8	7	2	9	6	10
3						
5						
6						
0						
4						

Learning objectives

- Know by heart multiplication facts up to 10×10 and corresponding division facts.
- Derive quickly addition and subtraction facts to 20.

© OUP: Copying permitted for purchasing school only.

UNIT 22 Extended Number Facts

Strategies
- use knowledge of basic number facts
- reorder to simplify (e.g. 79 + 8 = 70 + 9 + 8 = 70 + 17)
- to multiply by 10, 100 or 1000 move digits left
- to divide by 10, 100 or 1000 move digits right
- use knowledge of place value to estimate answer

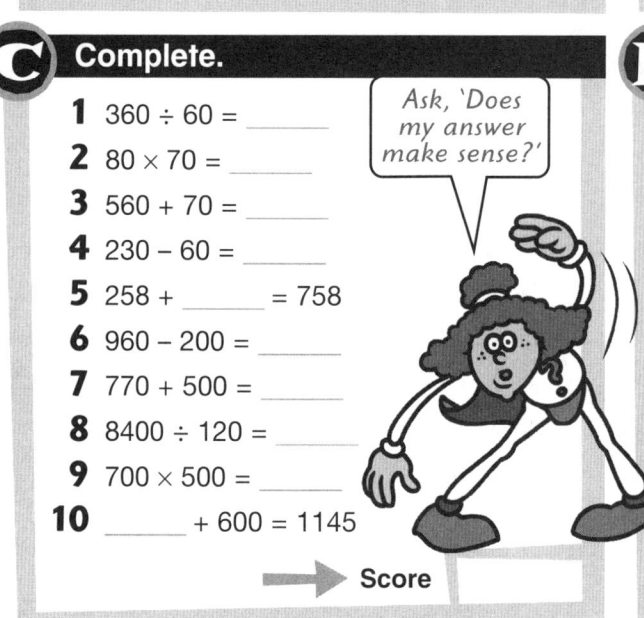

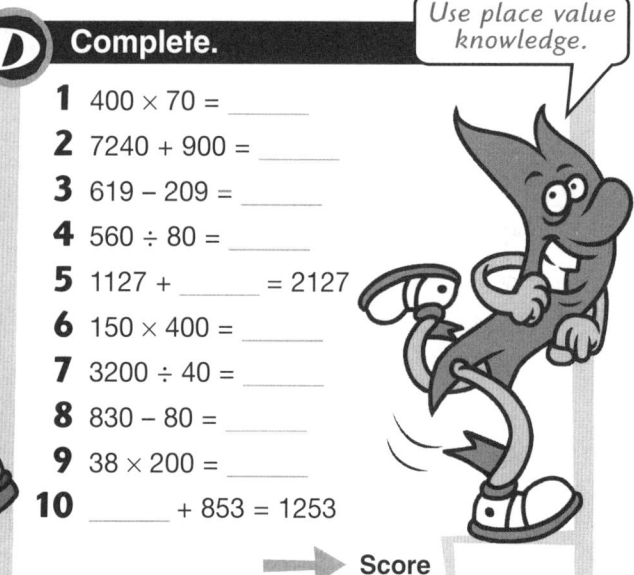

A Complete.
Try working backwards.

1. 76 + 9 = _____
2. 800 − 500 = _____
3. 60 × 7 = _____
4. 820 + 700 = _____
5. 240 ÷ 3 = _____
6. 50 × 20 = _____
7. 97 − 9 = _____
8. 2400 + 500 = _____
9. 700 ÷ 70 = _____
10. 15 000 − 7000 = _____

→ Score

B Complete.
Remember: estimate first.

1. 59 − 6 = _____
2. 475 − 225 = _____
3. 84 + 9 = _____
4. 442 + 205 = _____
5. 300 × 60 = _____
6. 673 − 253 = _____
7. 270 ÷ 90 = _____
8. 139 + 550 = _____
9. 340 × 10 = _____
10. 739 + _____ = 1339

→ Score

C Complete.
Ask, 'Does my answer make sense?'

1. 360 ÷ 60 = _____
2. 80 × 70 = _____
3. 560 + 70 = _____
4. 230 − 60 = _____
5. 258 + _____ = 758
6. 960 − 200 = _____
7. 770 + 500 = _____
8. 8400 ÷ 120 = _____
9. 700 × 500 = _____
10. _____ + 600 = 1145

→ Score

D Complete.
Use place value knowledge.

1. 400 × 70 = _____
2. 7240 + 900 = _____
3. 619 − 209 = _____
4. 560 ÷ 80 = _____
5. 1127 + _____ = 2127
6. 150 × 400 = _____
7. 3200 ÷ 40 = _____
8. 830 − 80 = _____
9. 38 × 200 = _____
10. _____ + 853 = 1253

→ Score

Listen and Write

1. _____
2. _____
3. _____
4. _____
5. _____
6. _____
7. _____
8. _____
9. _____
10. _____

→ Score

Think About It!

1. I am a three-digit number.
2. I am a square number.
3. I am divisible by 4.
4. The sum of my first and second digits is the same as the sum of my first and last digits.
5. The sum of all my digits is also a square number.
6. If you write me backwards, I am divisible by 3.
7. An old name for me is gross.
8. I am equivalent to a dozen dozens. _____

Learning objective
- Use known number facts and place value to calculate mentally.

UNIT 23 Measurement: Capacity

Strategies
- make the units of measurement the same
- use knowledge of basic number facts
- ask, 'Does my answer make sense?'
- learn the measurement tables

A Complete.
1. 650 ml + 340 ml = _____
2. 1.5 l + 2.5 l = _____
3. 8 l × 7 = _____
4. 500 ml × 7 = _____
5. 7.5 l + 700 ml = _____
6. 10 l – 3.8 l = _____
7. 500 ml @ £2.50 per litre = _____
8. 7200 ml = _____ l
9. 5.3 l = _____ ml
10. 500 ml ÷ 10 = _____

Score _____

If you × or +, the answer will be more.

B Complete.
1. 6.1 l – 400 ml = _____
2. 2.7 l + 800 ml = _____
3. 6.5 l × 5 = _____
4. 3000 ml ÷ 10 = _____
5. 5.25 l ÷ 10 = _____
6. 3.7 l + 300 ml + 6.2 l = _____
7. 250 ml @ £16.40 a litre = _____
8. 2.7 l ÷ 3 = _____
9. 750 ml × 3 = _____
10. 8.6 l = _____ ml

Score _____

If you ÷ or –, the answer will be less.

C Complete.
1. 3.6 l + 750 ml = _____
2. 6.2 l – 600 ml = _____
3. 800 ml × 9 = _____
4. 70p per litre. How much for $2\frac{1}{2}$ l? _____
5. 200 ml @ £20 per litre = _____
6. 15 l = _____ ml
7. $\frac{1}{2}$ of 5.6 l = _____
8. 7.1 l + 2.8 l + 500 ml = _____
9. 65.25 l ÷ 10 = _____
10. 475 ml × 10 = _____

Score _____

1000 ml = 1 l.

D Complete.
1. 550 ml + 5.5 l = _____
2. 16.5 l – 800 ml = _____
3. $\frac{1}{4}$ of 7.2 l = _____
4. 225 ml × 4 = _____
5. £1.20 per litre. How much for 250 ml? _____
6. 13.6 l ÷ 10 = _____
7. $\frac{1}{4}$ of 1 kilolitre? = _____ l
8. 750 ml @ £12 a litre = _____
9. 35.5 l ÷ 5 = _____
10. 5.7 l – 1300 ml = _____

Score _____

1000 l = 1 kilolitre.

Listen and Write
1 _____ 6 _____
2 _____ 7 _____
3 _____ 8 _____
4 _____ 9 _____
5 _____ 10 _____

Score _____

Think About It!

SoupaGuy is filling his 8 l bottles with his special SooperSoup.

He has 45.5 litres of SooperSoup. How many bottles will he fill and how much SooperSoup will be left over?

☐ bottles
☐ left over SooperSoup

Learning objectives
- Convert larger to smaller units.
- Solve simple problems involving measures (capacity).

UNIT 24 Equations

Strategies
- carry out operations one stage at a time
- work out one side of the equations first
- ask, 'Can I partition?'

Remember: try working backwards.

A Complete.

Remember: brackets first.

1. (10 + 20) × 6 = _____
2. 17 + 17 + 17 + 17 = 17 × _____
3. 39 × 8 = _____ × 8 – 8 = _____
4. (£50 – £18) + (£50 – £27) = _____
5. 32 × 5 = _____ × 10
6. 5 × 4 + 6 × 7 = _____
7. 81 ÷ (12 – 3) = _____
8. ($\frac{1}{4}$ of 16) × ($\frac{1}{3}$ of 9) = _____
9. (24 ÷ 4) × (32 ÷ 4) = _____
10. (7 + 3) × 6 – 8 = _____

➡ Score

B Complete.

1. $\frac{1}{2}$ of 32 = 4 × _____
2. (60 – 35) ÷ 5 = _____
3. 100 – (9 × 5) = _____
4. 18 × 5 × 6 = 30 × _____ + 30 × _____
5. ($\frac{1}{4}$ of 36) × ($\frac{1}{3}$ of 18) = _____
6. 16 + 16 + 16 + 16 + 16 = 10 × _____
7. (_____ + 40) × 7 = 700
8. (10 × 8) – (5 × 8) = _____ × 8 = _____
9. (7 + 8) – (24 ÷ 3) = _____
10. 14 × _____ = 7 × 20

➡ Score

C Complete.

Remember: = means that one side must be the same as the other side.

1. (7 + 9) × 3 = _____
2. (5 × 4) – (10 + 3) = _____
3. (5 × 4) × (10 – 3) = _____
4. (5 × 4) + (10 – 3) = _____
5. 48 ÷ (4² – 2²) = _____
6. ($\frac{1}{4}$ of 20) × ($\frac{1}{5}$ of 20) = _____
7. (8 + 9) – (42 ÷ 6) = _____
8. 800 = 40 × (16 + _____)
9. (5 × 5) + 100 = _____
10. (72 ÷ 9) × (28 ÷ 4) = _____

➡ Score

D Complete.

1. 10² = 10 × _____
2. 100 – (5 × 8) = _____
3. 18 ÷ 6 × $\frac{3}{4}$ of 20 = _____
4. (£50 – £26) + (£20 – £12) = _____
5. ($\frac{1}{3}$ of 18) × 10 = _____
6. 23 + 23 + 23 + 23 + 23 + 23 = 46 × _____
7. (200 × 3) + (40 × 3) + (7 × 3) = _____ × 3
8. 24 × 2 = 8 × _____ = 12 × _____
9. $\frac{1}{3}$ of 90 = 60 ÷ _____
10. (28 ÷ 4) × (36 ÷ 9) = _____

➡ Score

Listen and Write

1. _____ 6. _____
2. _____ 7. _____
3. _____ 8. _____
4. _____ 9. _____
5. _____ 10. _____

➡ Score

Think About It!

Batboy bought 72 Super Hero masks for £120.

If he sells the masks for £15 a dozen, what will be his profit or loss? _____

Learning objective
- Use appropriate number operations to solve problems.

41

© OUP: Copying permitted for purchasing school only.

UNIT 25 Counting and Order

Strategies
- ask, 'Which digits are repeating?'
- ask, 'Am I counting forwards or backwards?'
- ask, 'Is there more than one operation?'
- when ordering, visualise the Place Value chart

A Complete.

1. 18 23 28 _____ 38
2. 90 87 _____ 81 78
3. 62 66 70 74 _____
4. 0.5 1 1.5 _____ 2.5
5. 713 743 _____ 803 833
6. 25.4 25.2 25.0 24.8 _____
7. $\frac{1}{3}$ $\frac{2}{3}$ 1 _____ $1\frac{2}{3}$
8. 896 856 816 _____ 736
9. 2362 _____ 2962 3262 3562
10. 75.6 68.6 61.6 _____ 47.6

Score ____

Remember: if the numbers are getting larger, you must be counting forwards.

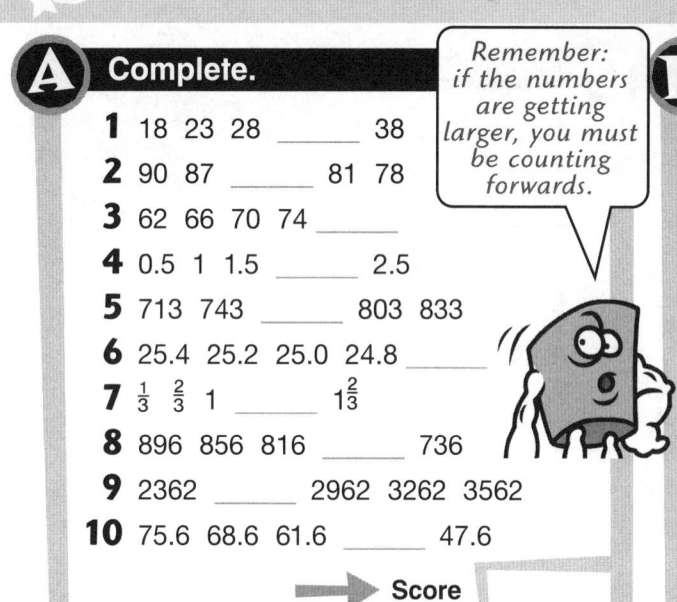

B Complete.

1. 1200 1800 2400 _____ 3600
2. 1.5 3.0 4.5 6 _____
3. 98 92 _____ 80 74
4. 3065 2765 2465 _____ 1865
5. 9053 8053 _____ 6053 5053
6. 55.4 60.4 65.4 _____ 75.4
7. $1\frac{1}{4}$ $1\frac{3}{4}$ _____ $2\frac{3}{4}$ $3\frac{1}{4}$
8. 5498 5438 5378 _____ 5258
9. 522.1 525.1 _____ 531.1 534.1
10. $\frac{1}{8}$ $\frac{3}{8}$ $\frac{5}{8}$ _____ $1\frac{1}{8}$

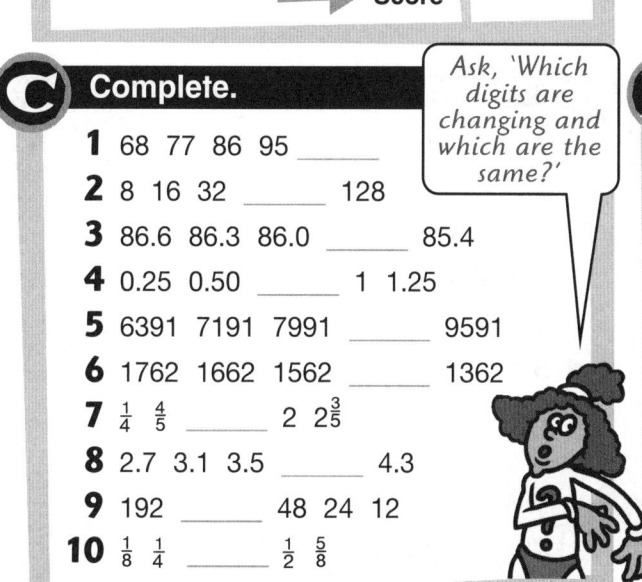

Score ____

Remember: if the numbers are getting smaller, you must be counting backwards.

C Complete.

1. 68 77 86 95 _____
2. 8 16 32 _____ 128
3. 86.6 86.3 86.0 _____ 85.4
4. 0.25 0.50 _____ 1 1.25
5. 6391 7191 7991 _____ 9591
6. 1762 1662 1562 _____ 1362
7. $\frac{1}{4}$ $\frac{4}{5}$ _____ 2 $2\frac{3}{5}$
8. 2.7 3.1 3.5 _____ 4.3
9. 192 _____ 48 24 12
10. $\frac{1}{8}$ $\frac{1}{4}$ _____ $\frac{1}{2}$ $\frac{5}{8}$

Score ____

Ask, 'Which digits are changing and which are the same?'

D Complete.

1. 896 89.6 _____ 0.896
2. 0.128 _____ 12.8 128
3. 80.04 8.004 _____ 0.08004
4. 0.116 1.16 11.6 _____
5. $\frac{3}{16}$ $\frac{3}{8}$ $\frac{9}{16}$ _____ $\frac{15}{16}$
6. 8500 8750 _____ 9250 9500
7. 25.25 25.75 26.25 _____ 27.25
8. 9635 9705 9775 _____ 9915
9. $\frac{2}{3}$ $\frac{1}{16}$ $1\frac{2}{3}$ _____ $2\frac{2}{3}$
10. 1769 2869 _____ 5069 6169

Score ____

Shifting the digits one place to the right decreases the value 10 times. Shifting the digits one place to the left increases the value 10 times.

Listen and Write

1 ____   6 ____
2 ____   7 ____
3 ____   8 ____
4 ____   9 ____
5 ____   10 ____

Score ____

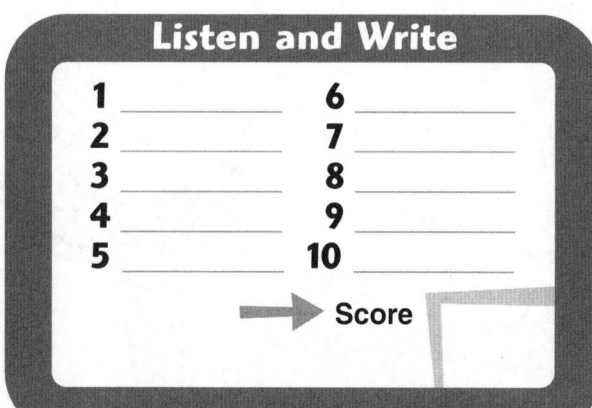

Think About It!

Write in order: smallest to largest.

110 101   111 001   101 010   111.101
101 001   101 001   110.101   101.101

_____
_____

Learning objective
- Recognise and extend number sequences.

Review 5

A Complete.
1. 8 + 9 = _____
2. 6 × 5 = _____
3. 24 ÷ 8 = _____
4. 12 − 5 = _____
5. 500 ml @ £7 per litre = _____
6. 900 − 500 = _____
7. ($\frac{1}{2}$ of 12) + ($\frac{1}{4}$ of 8) = _____
8. Next? 7 14 21 28 _____
9. 300 ml × 4 = _____
10. (4 × 3) + (7 × 2) = _____

→ Score

B Complete.
1. _____ + 6 = 13
2. 8 × _____ = 56
3. _____ ÷ 3 = 5
4. 13 − _____ = 6
5. 250 ml @ £4.40 a litre = _____
6. 2600 − 1300 = _____
7. (_____ + 30) × 8 = 800
8. Next? 1.6 2.4 3.2 _____
9. 45.5 l ÷ 5 = _____
10. 100 − (7 × 6) = _____

→ Score

C Complete.
1. 4 + _____ = 11
2. _____ × 9 = 27
3. 42 ÷ _____ = 7
4. _____ − 7 = 9
5. 750 ml @ £16 a litre = _____
6. 36 × 4 = 18 × _____ = 9 × _____
7. $\frac{1}{3}$ of 30 = 30 ÷ _____
8. Next? 2743 2703 2663 _____
9. 1.7 l + 650 ml = _____
10. 750 × 10 = _____

→ Score

D Complete.
1. 8 + 8 = _____
2. 54 = 6 × _____
3. 6 = _____ ÷ 8
4. 18 − 11 = _____
5. $2\frac{1}{2}$ l @ £1.80 a litre = _____
6. 60p a litre. How much for $6\frac{1}{2}$ l? _____
7. Next? $\frac{1}{3}$ $\frac{1}{2}$ $\frac{2}{3}$ $\frac{5}{6}$ _____
8. (70 − 20) ÷ ($\frac{1}{9}$ of 18) = _____
9. 600 × 900 = _____
10. $9^2 + 8^2 + 5^2$ = _____

→ Score

Listen and Write
1. _____   6. _____
2. _____   7. _____
3. _____   8. _____
4. _____   9. _____
5. _____   10. _____

→ Score

Think About It!
Try working backwards.

- Ribbon was paid on Monday.
- On Tuesday she spent £75 on a new pair of flying shoes.
- On Wednesday she spent £75 on SoupaFoods.
- On Thursday Batboy repaid the £50 he owed Ribbon.

If Ribbon now has £200, how much money was she paid on Monday? _____

Check-up
- I can derive quickly and use multiplication and division facts to 10 × 10.
- I can extend number sequences.
- I can use known number facts and place value to work out new facts, e.g. use 6 × 5 to find 60 × 50.

Take a Break

It's a Code and you can Quote Me!

Solve each problem then use the code to complete the famous quote.

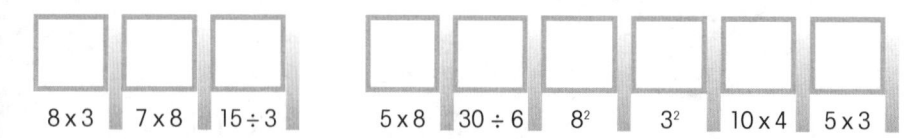

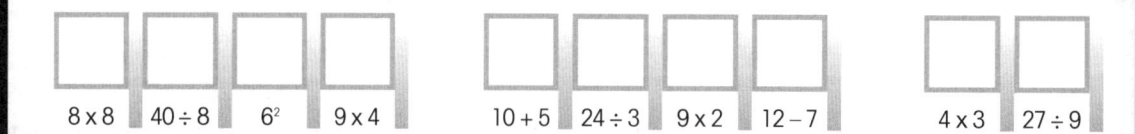

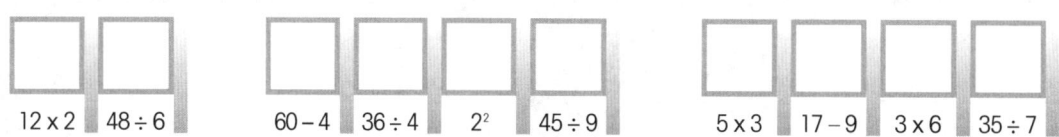

8 x 3	7 x 8	15 ÷ 3		5 x 8	30 ÷ 6	8^2	3^2	10 x 4	5 x 3

56 ÷ 7	21 ÷ 3		81 ÷ 9		6 x 4	8 x 7	20 − 8	6 x 3	5 x 6

8 x 8	40 ÷ 8	6^2	9 x 4		10 + 5	24 ÷ 3	9 x 2	12 − 7		4 x 3	27 ÷ 9

12 x 2	48 ÷ 6		60 − 4	36 ÷ 4	2^2	45 ÷ 9		5 x 3	17 − 9	3 x 6	35 ÷ 7

6 x 2 | 3 x 8   *Ralph Waldo Emerson*

A	D	E	F	G	H	I	L	N	O	R	S	T	V	W
9	15	5	7	30	56	12	36	18	8	40	3	24	4	64

Learning objectives
- Know by heart multiplication facts to 10 × 10 and derive quickly corresponding division facts.
- Derive quickly addition and subtraction facts.

UNIT 26 Number Facts

Strategies
- rearrange to simplify
- check by working backwards
- ask, 'Does my answer make sense?'
- break the number down to double or halve (e.g. double 57 = 100 + 14 = 114)

A Complete.

1. 64 ÷ 8 = _____
2. 7 × 5 = _____
3. Double 26 = _____
4. 12 − 7 = _____
5. _____ ÷ 7 = 7
6. Half of 38 = _____
7. 5 × _____ = 40
8. 3^2 = _____
9. 24 ÷ 6 = _____
10. 7 × 0 = _____

Remember: to double × 2.

Score ____

B Complete.

1. 7 + 6 = _____
2. 8 × 3 = _____
3. _____ ÷ 3 = 8
4. Half of 92 = _____
5. 36 ÷ 9 = _____
6. 8 × _____ = 56
7. 13 − 9 = _____
8. Double 17 = _____
9. 6^2 = _____
10. 48 ÷ 4 = _____

Remember: to halve ÷ 2.

Score ____

C Complete.

1. 7 × _____ = 49
2. Double 47 = _____
3. 9 × 4 = _____
4. 4^2 = _____
5. 56 ÷ 7 = _____
6. _____ ÷ 8 = 3
7. 10 × _____ = 100
8. 14 − 6 = _____
9. Half of 116 = _____
10. _____ + 8 = 17

Remember: + or × means the answer must be more; − or ÷ means the answer must be less.

Score ____

D Complete.

1. 18 − _____ = 8
2. 36 ÷ 6 = _____
3. 8^2 = _____
4. _____ ÷ 6 = 9
5. Double 77 = _____
6. Half of 236 = _____
7. 7 × 6 = _____
8. 81 ÷ _____ = 9
9. 8 + 4 = _____
10. 4 × _____ = 28

Try working backwards.

Score ____

Listen and Write

1. _____   6. _____
2. _____   7. _____
3. _____   8. _____
4. _____   9. _____
5. _____   10. _____

Score ____

Think About It!

1. How many bricks in a wall 8 bricks long and 9 bricks high? _____
2. Our journey was 63 km long and we stopped for a rest every 7 kilometres. How many stops did we make? _____
3. I had 17. I lost 9. How many do I have now? _____
4. 9 hats @ £6 each? _____

Learning objectives
- Know by heart multiplication facts to 10 × 10 and derive quickly corresponding division facts.
- Derive quickly doubles of numbers to at least 100 and corresponding halves.

45

© OUP: Copying permitted for purchasing school only.

Unit 27 Money

Strategies
- round up or down to estimate an answer
- use the 'shopkeeper's method' to give change (count on) (e.g. Had £2. Spent £1.20. So £1.20 + 20p (£1.40) + 10p (£1.50) + 50p (£2) = 80p change)
- ask, 'Does my answer make sense?'

A Complete.
Remember: 100p = £1.

1. £10 − 50p = _____
2. £2, how many 50p coins? _____
3. Pence in £1.35? _____
4. Had £10. Spent £2.50. _____ left
5. £6.35 + £3.20 = _____
6. 5 kg @ £1.50 per kilo = _____
7. £1, how many 20p coins? _____
8. Spent £2.40. Change from £5? = _____
9. $\frac{1}{4}$ of £12 = _____
10. 6 @ 40p each = _____

➡ Score _____

B Complete.
Ask, 'Will the answer be more or less?'

1. £20 − £15.45 = _____
2. £2, how many 10p coins? _____
3. Pence in £2.75? _____
4. Had £1. Spent 35p. _____ left
5. £7.50 − £1.25 = _____
6. 5 @ £2.50 = _____
7. £10, how many 20p coins? _____
8. Spent £8.65. Change from £10? = _____
9. $\frac{1}{5}$ of £20 = _____
10. 7 @ 25p each = _____

➡ Score _____

C Complete.
Remember: five 20p = £1.

1. £50 − £26.50 = _____
2. £5, how many 20p coins? _____
3. Pence in £3.15? = _____
4. £3.50 + £2.75 = _____
5. 500 g @ £1.50 a kilo = _____
6. £12.50, how many 10p? _____
7. Change from £10 if I spend £1.30? _____
8. 7 kg @ £8 per kg = _____
9. $\frac{1}{4}$ of £10 = _____
10. 3 @ £3.50 each = _____

➡ Score _____

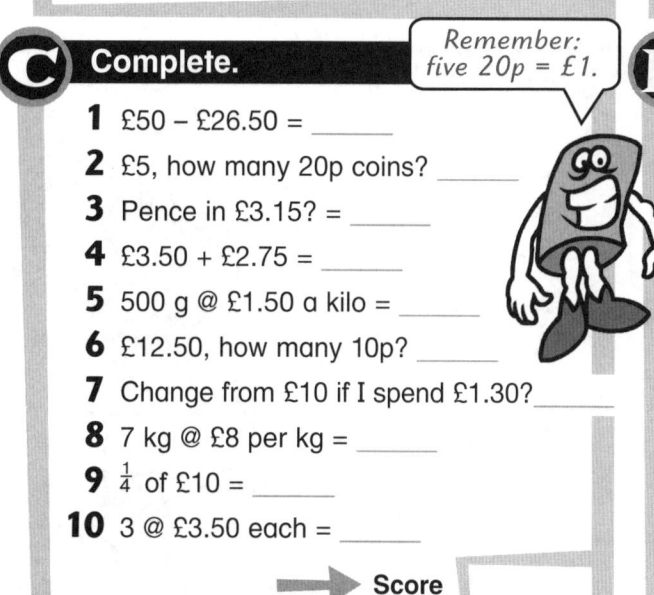

D Complete.
Remember: ten 10p = £1.

1. £10 − £7.35 = _____
2. £5, how many 10p coins? _____
3. 250 g @ £1.60 per kilo = _____
4. Spent £6.15. Change from £20? = _____
5. 500 ml @ £2.50 a litre = _____
6. Pence in £14.65? _____
7. £5.75 + £5.75 = _____
8. Change from £20 if I spend £13.45? _____
9. 9 @ 25p each = _____
10. $\frac{3}{5}$ of £20 = _____

➡ Score _____

Listen and Write

1. _____ 6. _____
2. _____ 7. _____
3. _____ 8. _____
4. _____ 9. _____
5. _____ 10. _____

➡ Score _____

Think About It!

- SoupaGuy saved £1.50 a day during June.
- WonderGal saved £16 a week for 3 weeks.
- Batboy saved £10 a fortnight for 8 weeks.
- Ribbon saved £13 a month from April to July.

Who saved the most? _____

Learning objective
- Solve problems involving money.

UNIT 28 Factors

Strategies
- use knowledge of basic number facts
- to find a missing factor divide the number by the factor (or factors) you have
  (e.g. 24 = __ × 6 = 24 ÷ 6 = 4 OR 72 = __ × 2 × 4 = 72 ÷ 2 = 36 ÷ 4 = 9)

A Complete.

Remember: a factor is a number that will divide equally into another number.

1. 30 = _____ × _____
2. 24 = _____ × _____
3. 16 = _____ × _____
4. 60 = _____ × _____
5. 18 = _____ × _____
6. 54 = _____ × _____
7. 45 = _____ × _____
8. 72 = _____ × _____
9. 12 = _____ × _____
10. 81 = _____ × _____

Score

B Complete.

Try working backwards.

1. 24 = 2 × 3 × _____
2. 12 = 2 × 2 × _____
3. 20 = 5 × 2 × _____
4. 18 = 3 × 3 × _____
5. 40 = 4 × 2 × _____
6. 64 = _____ × 4 × 2
7. 56 = _____ × 2 × 7
8. 100 = _____ × 5 × 2
9. 54 = _____ × 3 × 2
10. 30 = _____ × 3 × 2

Score

C Complete.

1. 18 = _____ × 2
2. 20 = 5 × _____
3. 48 = 6 × _____
4. 60 = 5 × _____ × 6
5. 108 = 4 × 3 × _____
6. 100 = 4 × 5 × _____
7. 24 = 2 × 4 × _____
8. 50 = _____ × 2 × 5
9. 12 = _____ × 1 × 2
10. 36 = 3 × _____ × 4

Score

D Complete.

1. 10 = 1 × 2 × _____
2. 16 = 4 × _____ × 2
3. 35 = 7 × _____
4. 72 = 4 × 2 × _____ × 3
5. 42 = 2 × _____ × 7
6. 28 = 2 × 2 × _____
7. 80 = 5 × 2 × 4 × _____
8. 72 = _____ × 6 × 2
9. 100 = 5 × 10 × _____
10. 81 = 3 × _____ × 3

Score

Listen and Write

1. _____   6. _____
2. _____   7. _____
3. _____   8. _____
4. _____   9. _____
5. _____   10. _____

Score

Think About It!

What number does each shape represent?

☆ × △ × △ = 16   ☐ × △ × ☆ = 24
○ × △ × ☐ = 30   ☆ × ○ × △ = 40
☐ × ☐ × ☐ = 27   △ × △ × △ = 8

☆ =   △ =   ☐ =   ○ =

Learning objective
- Find all the pairs of factors of any number up to 100.

Unit 29 Fractions and Decimals

Strategies
- to multiply or divide by 10, 100 or 1000 shift digits to the left (×) or right (÷)
- ask, 'Does my answer make sense?'
- to find a percentage make the denominator 100 (remember that whatever you do to the denominator you must also do to the numerator)

A Complete.

1. As a mixed number? $\frac{5}{2}$ = _____
2. As an improper fraction? $1\frac{3}{4}$ = _____
3. $\frac{1}{4}$ of 8 = _____
4. $\frac{1}{2}$ of 36 = _____
5. As a decimal? $\frac{7}{10}$ = _____
6. As a fraction? 0.5 = _____
7. 0.7 + 0.4 = _____
8. 0.9 − 0.3 = _____
9. $\frac{2}{5}$ of 10 = _____
10. $\frac{25}{100}$ = _____ %

→ Score

Remember: in an improper fraction the numerator will be larger than the denominator.

B Complete.

1. As a mixed number? $\frac{7}{3}$ = _____
2. As an improper fraction? $2\frac{1}{4}$ = _____
3. $\frac{1}{5}$ of 25 = _____
4. 1.25 + 2.75 = _____
5. As a decimal? $\frac{1}{4}$ = _____
6. As a fraction? 0.75 = _____
7. 8.4 − 1.6 = _____
8. $\frac{9}{10}$ of 40 = _____
9. $\frac{75}{100}$ = _____ %
10. As a fraction? 81% = _____

→ Score

Remember: a decimal point separates the whole number from the fractional part.

C Complete.

1. As a mixed number? $\frac{11}{4}$ = _____
2. As an improper fraction? $3\frac{2}{3}$ = _____
3. $\frac{2}{5}$ of 20 = _____
4. 0.9 + 3.8 = _____
5. As a decimal? $2\frac{1}{10}$ = _____
6. As a fraction? 3.7 = _____
7. 6.2 − 5.7 = _____
8. $\frac{4}{5}$ of 90 = _____
9. $\frac{30}{100}$ = _____ %
10. 10% of 90 = _____

→ Score

Remember: % means out of 100.

D Complete.

1. As a mixed number? $\frac{23}{6}$ = _____
2. As an improper fraction? $4\frac{3}{4}$ = _____
3. $\frac{5}{8}$ × 24 = _____
4. 2.5 + 1.75 = _____
5. As a decimal? $2\frac{3}{5}$ = _____
6. As a fraction? 9.5 = _____
7. 5.15 − 2.05 = _____
8. 6 × 1.2 = _____
9. $\frac{3}{4}$ = _____ %
10. 20% of 120 = _____

→ Score

Remember: numerator = top number, denominator = bottom number.

Listen and Write

1. _____   6. _____
2. _____   7. _____
3. _____   8. _____
4. _____   9. _____
5. _____   10. _____

→ Score

Think About It!

Change these test scores to percentages.
- SoupaGuy $\frac{20}{50}$ = _____ %
- Batboy $\frac{23}{25}$ = _____ %
- WonderGal $\frac{16}{20}$ = _____ %
- Ribbon $\frac{4}{5}$ = _____ %

Learning objectives
- Relate fractions to division to find simple fractions.
- Express fractions as decimals or percentages.

UNIT 30 Place Value

Strategies
- form a mental picture of the Place Value chart
- add digits of the same value

millions	thousands	units	10ths	100ths	1000ths
h t u	h t u	h t u			

Remember: although 0 has no value itself, its place affects the value of digits around it.

A Complete.

1. 60 + 80 000 + 400 + 2000 + 7 = _____
2. 70 + 7000 = _____
3. 2405 = _____ hundreds + 5 units
4. 6.3 = _____ units + 3
5. Value of 4 in 862 943? _____
6. 625.4 = 625 units + _____ tenths
7. 8324 = _____ tens + 4 units
8. 76 095 = 760 hundreds + _____
9. Value of 6 in 304.6? _____
10. 400 + 0.4 + 4000 + 4 = _____

→ Score

B Complete.

1. 1000 more than 7003 = _____
2. Value of 6 in 864 231.7? _____
3. 4 + 200 000 + 6000 + 90 + 50 000 = _____
4. Value of 24 in 98 246? _____
5. 833.24 = 833 units + 24 _____
6. 10 000 more than 25 652 = _____
7. 600 + 50 000 + 8 = _____
8. How many hundreds in 7500? _____
9. Value of 5 in 479.05? _____
10. 80 + 0.09 + 7 + 0.9 = _____

→ Score

C Complete.

1. 100 000 more than 276 539 = _____
2. 0.7 + 7000 + 700 = _____
3. Value of 3 in 362 549.25? _____
4. How many hundreds in 64 000? _____
5. Value of 17 in 86 317.05? _____
6. 100 000 less than 8 473 263 = _____
7. 80 000 + 9000 + 500 + 8 + 60 = _____
8. Value of 13 in 8.13? _____
9. Value of 8 in 6524.78? _____
10. $\frac{3}{10} + \frac{2}{100} + 80 + 600 + 9 =$ _____

→ Score

D Complete.

1. 50 + 50 000 + 0.05 + 600 + 0.7 = _____
2. Value of 1 in 8 124 267.5? _____
3. Value of 37 in 26.37? _____
4. 20 + 300 000 + 900 + 6000 = _____
5. 1 million more than 5 437 269 = _____
6. How many tens in 250 000? _____
7. $\frac{7}{100} + \frac{9}{10} + 4000 + 500 + 8 + 60 =$ _____
8. Value of 4 in 0.64? _____
9. 60 + 2 tenths + 800 + 0.09 = _____
10. 100 000 less than 1.8 million = _____

→ Score

Listen and Write

1. _____ 6. _____
2. _____ 7. _____
3. _____ 8. _____
4. _____ 9. _____
5. _____ 10. _____

→ Score

Think About It!

Rewrite the areas of these 5 National Parks in simpler terms.

Name	Area (ha)	Simpler term
Brecon Beacons	100 000 + 100 + 30 000 + 5000	
Exmoor	9000 + 80 + 60 000 + 200	
Lake District	200 + 200 000 + 9000 + 20 000	
Snowdonia	14 000 + 100 + 200 000 + 60	
Yorkshire Dales	800 + 100 000 + 70 + 76 000	

Learning objectives
- Read and write whole numbers in figures and words and know what each digit represents.
- Know what each digit represents in a number with up to two decimal places.

© OUP: Copying permitted for purchasing school only.

Review 6

A Complete.
1. 7 + 4 = _____
2. 6 × 4 = _____
3. 36 ÷ 9 = _____
4. 16 − 9 = _____
5. 6 @ 70p each = _____
6. 40 = _____ × _____
7. $\frac{1}{2} + \frac{1}{4}$ = _____
8. £5, how many 10p coins? _____
9. 6 × 0.3 = _____
10. 6 + 7000 + 500 + 90 = _____

Score ____

B Complete.
1. _____ + 8 = 15
2. 7 × _____ = 49
3. _____ ÷ 6 = 4
4. 15 − _____ = 4
5. 9 @ £1.20 each = _____
6. 24 = 3 × _____ × _____
7. As a decimal? $3\frac{2}{5}$ = _____
8. £10 − £3.85 = _____
9. $\frac{1}{5}$ × 8 = _____
10. 1000 more than 85 000 = _____

Score ____

C Complete.
1. 6 + _____ = 13
2. _____ × 4 = 28
3. 72 ÷ _____ = 8
4. _____ − 8 = 3
5. 3 @ £6.30 each = _____
6. 16 = 2 × _____ × _____
7. $\frac{40}{50}$ = _____ %
8. Change from £10 if I spend £1.65? _____
9. As a fraction? 0.7 = _____
10. Value of 3 in 862.43? _____

Score ____

D Complete.
1. 9 + 9 = _____
2. 30 = 5 × _____
3. 8 = _____ ÷ 7
4. 17 − 9 = _____
5. 250 kg @ £3.60 a kilo = _____
6. 56 = 2 × _____ × 7
7. $\frac{1}{3} + \frac{1}{2}$ = _____
8. $\frac{2}{5}$ of £30 = _____
9. 10% of £70 = _____
10. 70 + $\frac{3}{10}$ + $\frac{5}{100}$ + 6 = _____

Score ____

Listen and Write
1. _____   6. _____
2. _____   7. _____
3. _____   8. _____
4. _____   9. _____
5. _____   10. _____

Score ____

Think About It!
To get to his latest rescue SoupaGuy travelled 240 km in 10 minutes.

What speed did SoupaGuy average in km/h?

_____ km/h

Check-up
- I can recognise the value of each digit in a whole or decimal number.
- I can use fractions of numbers to multiply.
- I can find simple fractions of number and quantities.

Take a Break 6

Use the problems below to help you solve this CROSSNUMBER.

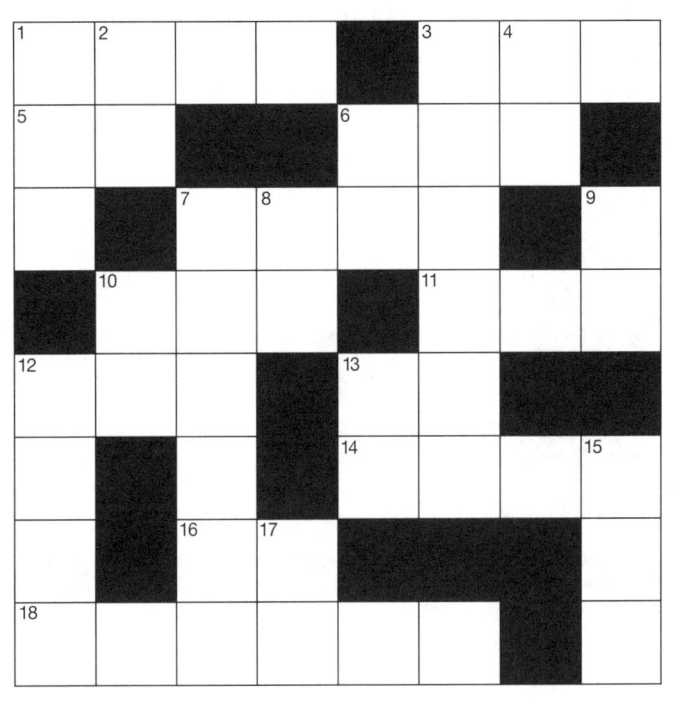

Across

1 70 × 80
3 A dozen dozens
5 6 × 4
6 12 × 9
7 Pence in £12.40?
10 0.6 l = _____ ml
11 30² =
12 (60 × 4) + (7 × 3)
13 1200 ÷ 40
14 66 hundreds + 6
16 Double 3²
18 Half of 1 million

Down

1 1000 – 475
2 8²
3 100 000 + 6 + 900
4 6 × 8
6 56 ÷ 4
7 100 000 + 10 + 1000
8 5 × 4
9 10% of 100
10 11 × 6
12 995 mm + 2 metres
     = _____ mm
13 6²
15 (80 × 8) + (12 × 5) – 5
17 9² – 1

Learning objectives

- Use known number facts and place value to calculate mentally.
- Use doubling and halving.
- Know squares of numbers to at least 10 × 10.

Unit 31 Number Facts

Strategies
- odd × odd = even
- even × even = even
- odd × even = even
- even ÷ even = odd
- even ÷ odd = even
- odd ÷ odd = odd

A Complete.

1. 6 × 4 = _____
2. 7 × 3 = _____
3. 5 × 6 = _____
4. 24 ÷ 3 = _____
5. 35 ÷ 7 = _____
6. 8 + 7 = _____
7. _____ − 6 = 9
8. _____ ÷ 4 = 12
9. 6 × _____ = 48
10. 5^2 = _____

Remember: multiplication is the same as repeated addition.

→ Score

B Complete.

1. 8 × 5 = _____
2. 6 × 9 = _____
3. _____ × 4 = 32
4. 18 ÷ 3 = _____
5. 64 ÷ _____ = 8
6. _____ + 6 = 15
7. 13 − _____ = 7
8. 28 ÷ _____ = 7
9. 4 × _____ = 16
10. 9^2 = _____

Remember: division is the same as repeated subtraction.

→ Score

C Complete.

1. _____ × 4 = 40
2. 45 ÷ 9 = _____
3. 6 + _____ = 17
4. 10^2 = _____
5. _____ − 8 = 4
6. 7 × _____ 21
7. _____ ÷ 7 = 5
8. 14 − _____ = 7
9. 8 + _____ = 13
10. 8 × 6 = _____

Remember: if 7 + 6 = 13 then 13 − 6 = 7 and 13 − 7 = 6.

→ Score

D Complete.

1. _____ ÷ 6 = 9
2. 8 + _____ = 15
3. _____ × 3 = 27
4. 17 − 11 = _____
5. 6^2 = _____
6. 16 − 9 = _____
7. 7 × 5 = _____
8. _____ + 9 = 14
9. 36 ÷ 3 = _____
10. 12 × _____ = 60

Remember: if A × B = C then C ÷ B = A and C ÷ A = B.

→ Score

Listen and Write

1. _____   6. _____
2. _____   7. _____
3. _____   8. _____
4. _____   9. _____
5. _____ 10. _____

→ Score

Think About It!

Complete the rule, then write the missing numbers.

a Subtract _____ then multiply by _____

11	12	9	6	8	10	5	7
27	30						

b Add _____ then divide by _____

3	9	6	15	12	21	18	30
3	5						

Learning objectives
- Know by heart multiplication facts up to 10 × 10 and derive quickly corresponding division facts.
- Derive quickly addition and subtraction facts to 20.

UNIT 32 Square Numbers

Strategies
- to square a number multiply the number by itself
- to find the square of a number find 2 factors that are the same
- learn the squares of numbers from 1 to 15

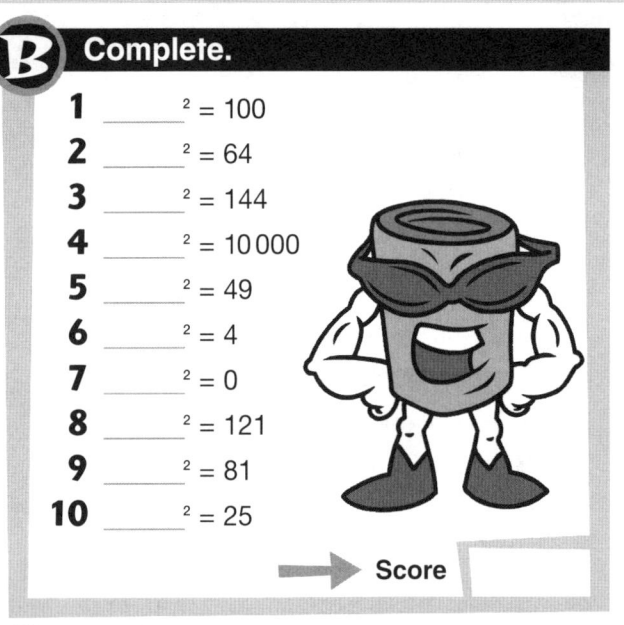

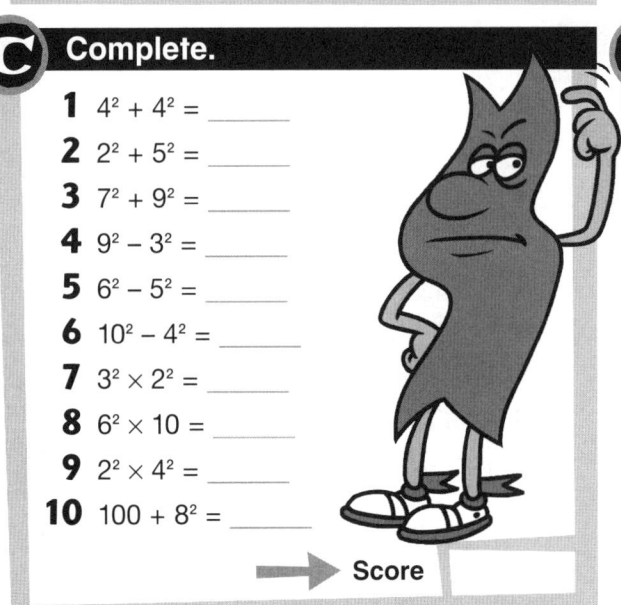

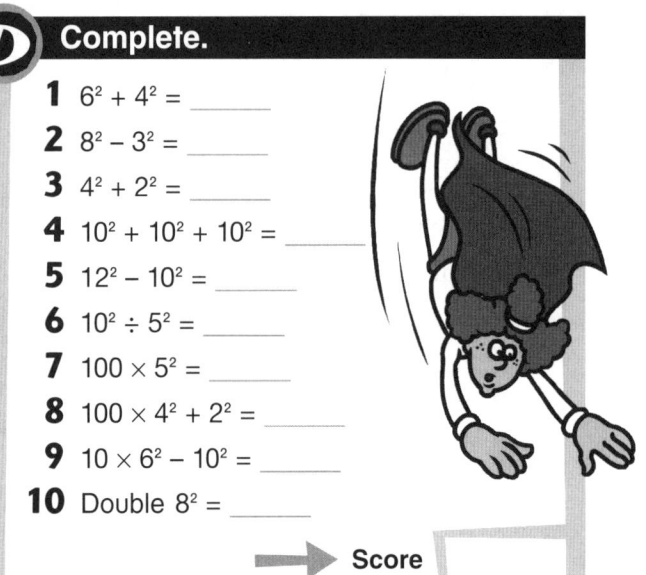

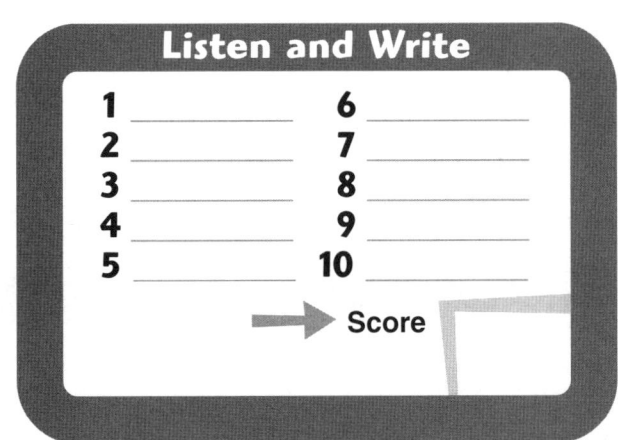

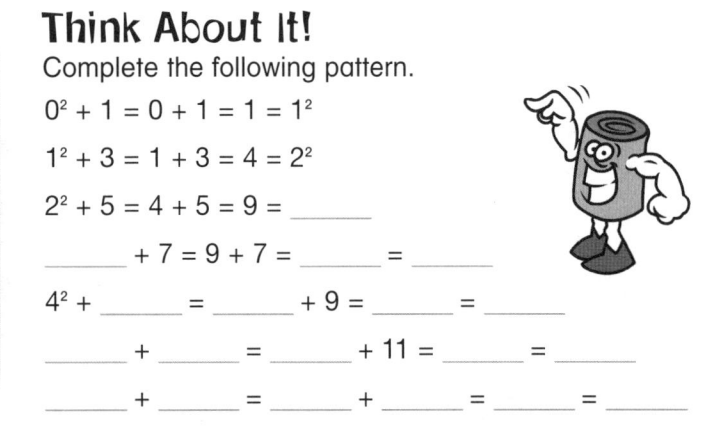

A Complete.

1. $2^2 = $ _____
2. $10^2 = $ _____
3. $5^2 = $ _____
4. $4^2 = $ _____
5. $8^2 = $ _____
6. $6^2 = $ _____
7. $9^2 = $ _____
8. $7^2 = $ _____
9. $3^2 = $ _____
10. $100^2 = $ _____

Remember: don't confuse squaring with doubling.

→ Score

B Complete.

1. ____$^2 = 100$
2. ____$^2 = 64$
3. ____$^2 = 144$
4. ____$^2 = 10\,000$
5. ____$^2 = 49$
6. ____$^2 = 4$
7. ____$^2 = 0$
8. ____$^2 = 121$
9. ____$^2 = 81$
10. ____$^2 = 25$

→ Score

C Complete.

1. $4^2 + 4^2 = $ _____
2. $2^2 + 5^2 = $ _____
3. $7^2 + 9^2 = $ _____
4. $9^2 - 3^2 = $ _____
5. $6^2 - 5^2 = $ _____
6. $10^2 - 4^2 = $ _____
7. $3^2 \times 2^2 = $ _____
8. $6^2 \times 10 = $ _____
9. $2^2 \times 4^2 = $ _____
10. $100 + 8^2 = $ _____

→ Score

D Complete.

1. $6^2 + 4^2 = $ _____
2. $8^2 - 3^2 = $ _____
3. $4^2 + 2^2 = $ _____
4. $10^2 + 10^2 + 10^2 = $ _____
5. $12^2 - 10^2 = $ _____
6. $10^2 \div 5^2 = $ _____
7. $100 \times 5^2 = $ _____
8. $100 \times 4^2 + 2^2 = $ _____
9. $10 \times 6^2 - 10^2 = $ _____
10. Double $8^2 = $ _____

→ Score

Listen and Write

1. _____ 6. _____
2. _____ 7. _____
3. _____ 8. _____
4. _____ 9. _____
5. _____ 10. _____

→ Score

Think About It!

Complete the following pattern.

$0^2 + 1 = 0 + 1 = 1 = 1^2$

$1^2 + 3 = 1 + 3 = 4 = 2^2$

$2^2 + 5 = 4 + 5 = 9 = $ _____

_____ $+ 7 = 9 + 7 = $ _____ $= $ _____

$4^2 + $ _____ $= $ _____ $+ 9 = $ _____ $= $ _____

_____ $+ $ _____ $= $ _____ $+ 11 = $ _____ $= $ _____

_____ $+ $ _____ $= $ _____ $+ $ _____ $= $ _____ $= $ _____

Learning objective
- Know squares of numbers to at least 10×10.

53

© OUP: Copying permitted for purchasing school only.

UNIT 33 Measurement: Time

Strategies
- make units the same
- speed × time = distance (e.g. 70 km/h for 4 hrs = 280 km)
- distance ÷ speed = time (e.g. 280 km at 70 km/h = 4 hours)
- distance ÷ time = speed (e.g. 280 km for 4 hrs = 70 km/h)

A Complete.
1. $3\frac{1}{4}$ hours = _____ minutes
2. 10 km at 20 km/h = _____ hour
3. Minutes from 8:30 a.m. to 9:15 a.m.? _____
4. 75 seconds = _____ mins _____ secs
5. Days in 7 weeks? _____
6. $2\frac{1}{2}$ hrs + $1\frac{1}{4}$ hrs = _____ mins
7. Years in 4 decades? _____
8. 3:45 + quarter of an hour = _____
9. 2:15 + 45 mins = _____
10. 9:55 + 40 mins = _____

→ Score

B Complete.
1. $7\frac{1}{2}$ hours = _____ minutes
2. 60 km/h for 9 hours = _____ km
3. Minutes from 2:15 pm to 2:55 pm = _____
4. 180 seconds = _____ mins _____ secs
5. $3\frac{3}{4}$ hrs + $2\frac{1}{2}$ hrs = _____ mins
6. 7:30 + 35 mins = _____
7. $7\frac{1}{2}$ centuries = _____ years
8. 11:25 + half an hour = _____
9. Days in June? _____
10. 7:20 + 55 mins = _____

→ Score

C Complete.
1. $5\frac{3}{4}$ hours = __ mins
2. 12 km/h for 3 hours = _____
3. Minutes from 1:30 a.m. to 2:05 a.m.? _____
4. 1.5 hours before noon = _____
5. Days in 2 fortnights? = _____
6. $5\frac{1}{2}$ mins + $3\frac{1}{2}$ mins = _____ seconds
7. 925 years = _____ centuries
8. 1:35 less $\frac{1}{4}$ of an hour = _____
9. 360 minutes = __ hours
10. 6:55 + 10 mins = _____

→ Score

D Complete.
1. $12\frac{1}{4}$ hours = _____ mins
2. 240 km in 4 hours = _____ km/h
3. Minutes from 11:45 a.m. to 12:35 p.m. = _____
4. 490 minutes = _____ hrs _____ mins
5. Days in March and April? _____
6. 10:25 + 50 mins = _____
7. $7\frac{3}{4}$ mins + $2\frac{1}{2}$ mins = _____ secs
8. 9:55 less $\frac{1}{2}$ an hour = _____
9. 140 years = _____ decades
10. 2.5 hrs before midnight = _____

→ Score

Listen and Write
1 _____ 6 _____
2 _____ 7 _____
3 _____ 8 _____
4 _____ 9 _____
5 _____ 10 _____

→ Score

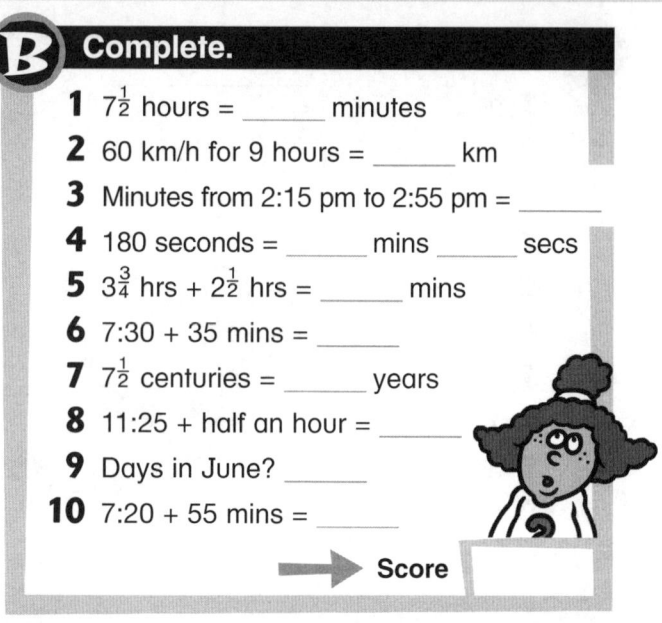

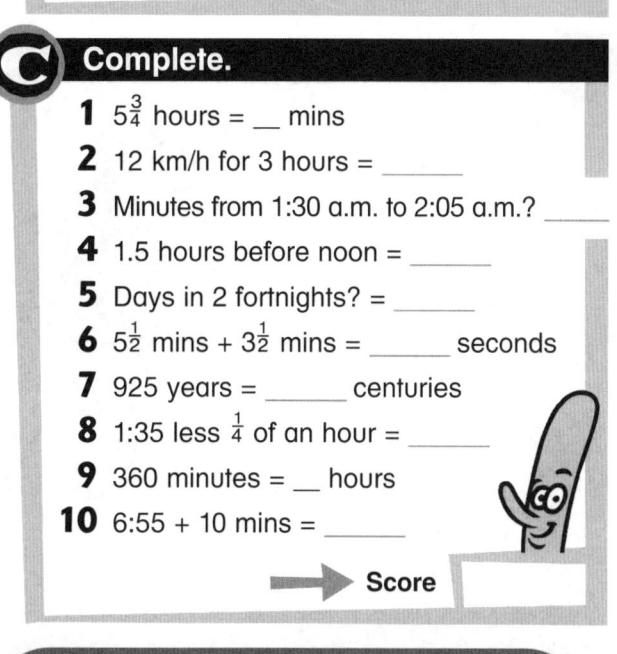

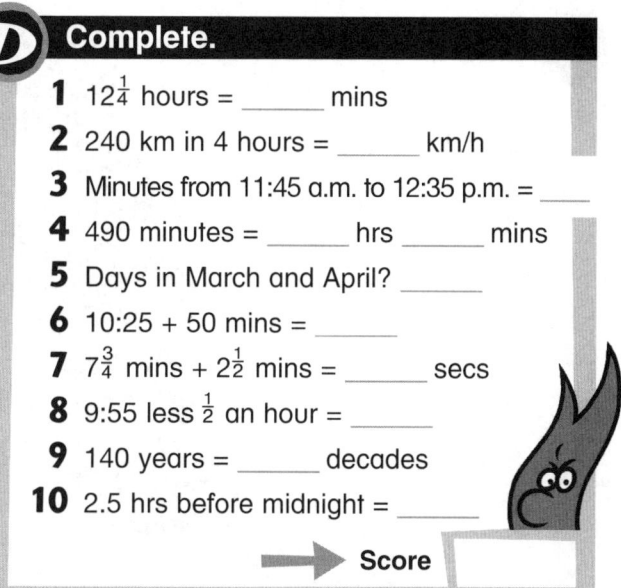

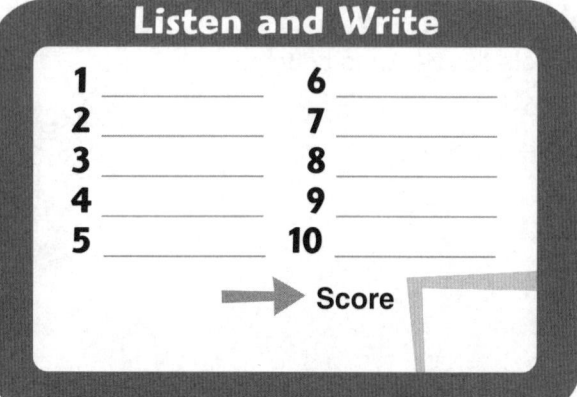

Think About It!

SoupaGuy doesn't know it but his watch loses 8 seconds every hour.

If it is 6 a.m. now and SoupaGuy has an appointment with Dr Ima Madscientist at 3:30 p.m. how late will SoupaGuy be?

(Write your answer in two different ways.)

Learning objectives
- Solve problems involving time.
- Use units of time.

UNIT 34 Counting and Order

Strategies
- ask, 'Which digits are repeating?'
- ask, 'Am I counting forwards or backwards?'
- ask, 'Is there more than one operation?'
- try working backwards

A Complete.
Are the numbers getting larger or smaller?

1. 17 22 27 _____ 37
2. 78 89 100 111 _____
3. 8.6 9.3 10.0 _____ 11.4
4. 659 650 _____ 632 623
5. 3421 3021 _____ 2221 1821
6. 863 913 963 _____ 1063
7. $\frac{1}{4}$ $\frac{1}{2}$ $\frac{3}{4}$ _____ $1\frac{1}{4}$
8. _____ 256 128 64 32
9. $\frac{1}{3}$ 1 $1\frac{2}{3}$ $2\frac{1}{3}$ _____
10. 2504 2564 2624 _____ 2744

Score _____

B Complete.
Do I add on or take off?

1. 87 76 65 54 _____
2. 26.4 29.4 32.4 _____ 38.4
3. 375 435 _____ 555 615
4. $\frac{3}{16}$ $\frac{5}{16}$ $\frac{7}{16}$ _____ $\frac{11}{16}$
5. 7764 8464 9164 _____ 10 564
6. 62.35 60.35 58.35 56.35 _____
7. $3\frac{3}{4}$ 3 $2\frac{1}{4}$ _____ $\frac{3}{4}$
8. _____ 288 144 72 36
9. 0.25 0.75 _____ 1.75 2.25
10. 32 420 37 420 _____ 47 420 52 420

Score _____

C Complete.
Which digits are changing and which are staying the same?

1. $\frac{3}{8}$ $\frac{3}{4}$ $1\frac{1}{8}$ $1\frac{1}{2}$ _____
2. 68.3 79.3 90.3 101.3 _____
3. 862 932 _____ 1072 1142
4. $\frac{1}{4}$ $1\frac{1}{2}$ $2\frac{3}{4}$ _____ $5\frac{1}{4}$
5. 5206 5166 _____ 5086 5046
6. 5.05 5.1 _____ 5.2 5.25
7. 3287 _____ 4087 4487 4887
8. 8649 8642 8635 _____ 8621
9. 597.3 598.1 598.9 599.7 _____
10. 352 176 88 _____ 22

Score _____

D Complete.
What is the pattern?

1. 2.1 4.2 8.4 _____ 33.6
2. $\frac{1}{6}$ $\frac{1}{2}$ $\frac{5}{6}$ $1\frac{1}{6}$ _____
3. 4375 4435 _____ 4555 4615
4. £18.50 £16 £13.50 £11 _____
5. $\frac{1}{8}$ $\frac{5}{16}$ $\frac{1}{2}$ _____ $\frac{7}{8}$
6. 72 908 _____ 60 908 54 908 48 908
7. 9950 9900 9850 _____ 9750
8. 49 64 81 _____ 121
9. 0.500 0.625 _____ 0.875 1
10. 1000.7 100.07 _____ 1.0007 0.10007

Score _____

Listen and Write

1. _____   6. _____
2. _____   7. _____
3. _____   8. _____
4. _____   9. _____
5. _____   10. _____

Score _____

Think About It!

Continue these counting patterns.

a Begin at 17. Count by 8s until you reach 105.
   17 _____

b Begin at 8.6. Count by 1.2 until you reach 23.
   8.6 _____

c Begin at 9462. Count backwards by 70s until you reach 8902.
   9462 _____

Learning objective
- Recognise and extend number sequences.

UNIT 35 Equations

Strategies
- work out one side of the equation first
- do one step at a time
- try reorganising the equation...but be careful not to change it

A Complete.
Remember: brackets first.

1. (5 + 10) × 20 = _____
2. 64 ÷ (4 × 2) = _____
3. (8 + 6) × 5 = 8 × 5 + _____ × _____
4. (£20 − £15) + (£20 − £10) + (£20 − £6) = _____
5. ($\frac{1}{3}$ of 27) × ($\frac{1}{5}$ of 40) = _____
6. 15 + 15 + 15 + 15 + 15 + 15 = 15 × _____
7. 57 × 9 = (50 × 9) + (_____ × 9)
8. (8 + 7) × (6 − 3) = _____
9. 60 ÷ ($\frac{1}{5}$ of 25) = _____
10. 100 − (8 × 3) = _____

→ Score

B Complete.
Remember: make one side of = the same as the other side.

1. (12 × 4) ÷ 4 = _____
2. (10 × 25) + (15 × 25) = _____ × 25
3. ($\frac{3}{4}$ of 40) + ($\frac{3}{4}$ of 8) = _____
4. (_____ + 20) × 9 = 900
5. 28 + 28 + 28 = 14 × _____
6. 4 × 27 × 5 = 20 × _____
7. (42 ÷ 7) × (36 ÷ 4) = _____
8. (7 − 3) × (8 + 2) = _____
9. (50 − 26) ÷ 3 = _____
10. $\frac{1}{2}$ of 36 = 6 × _____

→ Score

C Complete.
Remember: use your knowledge of basic number facts.

1. 42 ÷ (14 − 7) = _____
2. (27 ÷ 3) × (32 ÷ 4) = _____
3. (£10 − £6) + (£10 − £3) + (£10 − £5) = _____
4. 24 + 24 + 24 + 24 = 12 × _____
5. ($\frac{1}{6}$ of 36) × ($\frac{1}{4}$ of 24) = _____
6. $\frac{1}{4}$ of 48 = 3 × _____
7. 8 × _____ = (8 × 7) + (8 × 40) = _____
8. (100 − 48) × 3 = _____
9. (5 × 4) ÷ (10 ÷ 2) = _____
10. (17 − 9) × (5 + 4) = _____

→ Score

D Complete.
Ask, 'Can I make the equation more simple?'

1. (19 − 8) × 5 = _____
2. 70 ÷ (35 ÷ 5) = _____
3. (3 + 8) × (16 − 8) = _____
4. 36 + 36 + 36 + 36 = 8 × _____ = 9 × _____
5. (0 ÷ 5) × 25 = _____
6. ($\frac{3}{5}$ of 50) × ($\frac{2}{5}$ of 20) = _____
7. 7 × 16 × 10 = 70 × _____ = 160 × _____
8. 6 × £1.50 + 8 × £1.50 = _____
9. 2 × 2 × 2 × 8 = _____ × 8
10. (72 ÷ 6) ÷ 4 = _____

→ Score

Listen and Write

1. _____   6. _____
2. _____   7. _____
3. _____   8. _____
4. _____   9. _____
5. _____   10. _____

→ Score

Think About It!

1. How many £40 books for £400? _____
2. If I can buy 20 for £15, how many for £12? _____
3. How much for 1000 bricks at £32 per hundred? _____
4. If a woman has her 50th birthday this year in which year was she born? _____

Learning objective: Use appropriate number operations and ways of calculating.

Review 7

A Complete.
1. 8 + 5 = _____ 
2. 3 × 9 = _____
3. 25 ÷ 5 = _____
4. 17 − 8 = _____
5. 7^2 = _____
6. $5\frac{1}{4}$ hours = _____ minutes
7. Next? 5 10 20 40 _____
8. (4 × 9) − (5 × 7) = _____
9. 15 km/h for 4 hours = _____
10. $\frac{3}{4}$ of 12 × $\frac{1}{2}$ of 18 = _____

→ Score

B Complete.
1. _____ + 7 = 14
2. 6 × _____ = 30
3. _____ ÷ 7 = 4
4. 12 − _____ = 5
5. _____ ^{2} = 81
6. Minutes from 1:30 p.m. to 3:05 p.m.? _____
7. Next? 224 215 206 _____
8. (£5 − £2) + (£10 − £8) + (£20 − £6) = _____
9. $6\frac{1}{2}$ decades = _____ years
10. 16+16+16+16+16+16 = 8 × _____

→ Score

C Complete.
1. 6 + _____ = 15
2. _____ × 7 = 21
3. 60 ÷ _____ = 12
4. _____ − 6 = 11
5. $6^2 + 8^2$ = _____
6. 360 km in 3 hours = _____ km/h
7. Next? $\frac{1}{8}$ $\frac{3}{8}$ $\frac{5}{8}$ $\frac{7}{8}$ _____
8. ($\frac{1}{5}$ of 25) × ($\frac{1}{3}$ of 21) = _____
9. 2:05 less $\frac{1}{4}$ of an hour = _____
10. (100 − 46) ÷ 9 = _____

→ Score

D Complete.
1. 8 + 8 = _____
2. 54 = 9 × _____
3. 9 = _____ ÷ 5
4. 14 − 6 = _____
5. $12^2 − 5^2$ = _____
6. Days in 6 fortnights? = _____
7. Next? 9165 9105 9045 _____
8. (7 + 9) × ($\frac{1}{3}$ of 30) = _____
9. 550 minutes = _____ hrs _____ mins
10. 8 × 17 × 10 = _____ × 17 = _____

→ Score

Listen and Write
1. _____   6. _____
2. _____   7. _____
3. _____   8. _____
4. _____   9. _____
5. _____   10. _____

→ Score

Think About It!

Work out the rule and then complete each triangle.

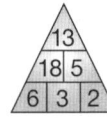

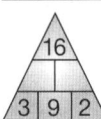

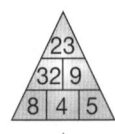

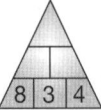

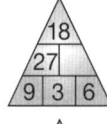

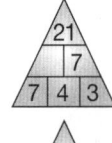

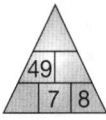

Triangle 1: 13 at top; 18, 5 middle; 6, 3, 2 bottom
Triangle 2: 23 at top; 32, 9 middle; 8, 4, 5 bottom
Triangle 3: 18 at top; 27 middle; 9, 3, 6 bottom
Triangle 4: 21 at top; 7 middle; 7, 4, 3 bottom
Triangle 5: 16 at top; 3, 9, 2 bottom
Triangle 6: 1 middle; 8, 3, 4 bottom
Triangle 7: 20 middle; 5, 5 bottom
Triangle 8: 49 middle; 7, 8 bottom

Check-up
- I can derive quick squares of numbers to at least 10.
- I know and can use the relationship between units of time.
- I can work through simple multi-step calculations.

57

© OUP: Copying permitted for purchasing school only.

Take a Break 7

How quickly and accurately can you complete each SoopaGrid?

QUICK GRID 1

+	9	4	6	5	1	8	7
7							
2							
8							
3							
0							
10							
9							

LADDER GRID

+	×	
9	3	
4	8	
7	7	
8	6	
4	5	
6	3	
9	5	
8	10	
4	9	
7	8	

WEB GRID

(web grid with × in center, numbers: 2, 4, 9, 6, 5, 7, 8, 9, 3, 8, 10, 4, 3, 5, 0, 8, 6, 9, 3, 6, 8, 7, 5)

QUICK GRID 2

×	8	2	3	5	0	7	9
3							
2							
4							
8							
10							
6							
7							

Learning objectives
- Know by heart multiplication facts up to 10 × 10.
- Derive quickly addition facts to 20.

© OUP: Copying permitted for purchasing school only.

UNIT 36 Number Facts

Strategies
- rearrange, partition, reorder to simplify
- check by working backwards
- ask, 'Does my answer make sense?'

A Complete.

1. 12 ÷ 3 = _____
2. 7 × _____ = 28
3. 7 + _____ = 16
4. 16 ÷ _____ = 4
5. _____ − 5 = 9
6. 16 − 8 = _____
7. 5 × 5 = _____
8. 20 ÷ _____ = 5
9. 12 − 9 = _____
10. _____ × 3 = 21

Remember:
odd + odd = even
even + even = even
odd + even = odd
even + odd = odd.

→ Score

B Complete.

1. 24 ÷ _____ = 4
2. 8 × 6 = _____
3. 7 + 6 = _____
4. _____ − 5 = 12
5. 18 ÷ _____ = 3
6. 5 × _____ = 35
7. _____ × 4 = 36
8. 13 − 9 = _____
9. _____ ÷ 5 = 8
10. _____ + 8 = 17

Remember:
odd − odd = even
even − even = even
odd − even = odd
even − odd = odd.

→ Score

C Complete.

1. 36 ÷ _____ = 6
2. _____ ÷ 4 = 8
3. 7 × 6 = _____
4. 8 + 6 = _____
5. 28 ÷ 7 = _____
6. 15 − _____ = 9
7. 8 × 7 = _____
8. 64 ÷ 8 = _____
9. _____ + 6 = 13
10. 9 × _____ = 72

Remember:
odd × odd = odd
odd ÷ odd = odd.

→ Score

D Complete.

1. 7 × _____ = 49
2. 8 + 9 = _____
3. _____ × 3 = 24
4. 81 ÷ _____ = 9
5. _____ − 7 = 9
6. 4 × _____ = 36
7. _____ + 8 = 15
8. 54 ÷ 6 = _____
9. 14 − _____ = 5
10. _____ ÷ 8 = 7

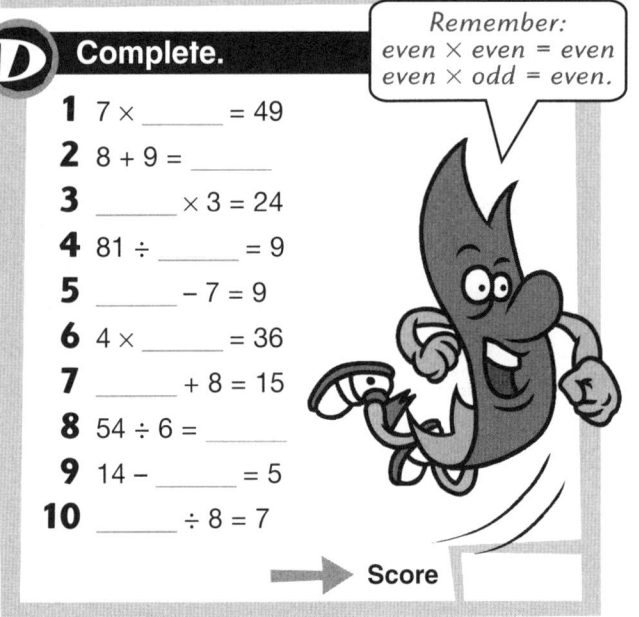

Remember:
even × even = even
even × odd = even.

→ Score

Listen and Write

1. _____   6. _____
2. _____   7. _____
3. _____   8. _____
4. _____   9. _____
5. _____   10. _____

→ Score

Think About It!

Complete these Y frames.

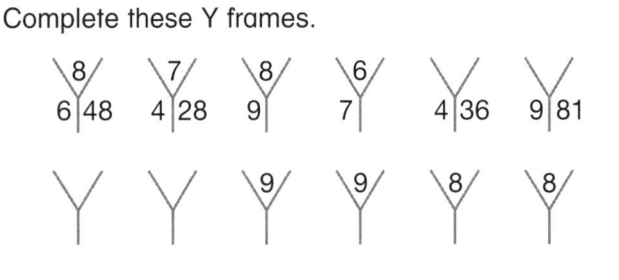

\8/   \7/   \8/   \6/   \ /   \ /
6|48 4|28 9| |7   4|36 9|81

\ /   \ /   \9/   \9/   \8/   \8/
 Y   Y   Y   Y   Y   Y

Learning objectives
- Know by heart multiplication facts up to 10 × 10 and derive quickly corresponding division facts.
- Derive quickly addition and subtraction facts to 20.

UNIT 37 Area and Perimeter

- to find P (perimeter) add the length of all sides
- to find P of a square multiply the length of one side by 4
- to find A (area) multiply the length (L) by the width (W)

A Perimeter of a square with sides...

Remember: the perimeter is the distance around a shape.

1. 4 cm? _____
2. 9 cm? _____
3. 6 cm? _____
4. 7 m? _____
5. 11 mm? _____
6. 20 m? _____
7. 10 cm? _____
8. 3 m? _____
9. 8 m? _____
10. 5 cm? _____

Score

B Perimeter of these rectangles?

Remember: area = L × W.

1. L = 3 m   W = 2 m   P = _____
2. L = 5 cm   W = 4 cm   P = _____
3. L = 8 m   W = 3 m   P = _____
4. L = 6 cm   W = 3 cm   P = _____
5. L = 9 m   W = 4 m   P = _____
6. L = 5 m   W = 2 m   P = _____
7. L = 40 m   W = 17 m   P = _____
8. L = 18 cm   W = 4 cm   P = _____
9. L = 30 cm   W = 24 cm   P = _____
10. L = 25 m   W = 15 m   P = _____

Score

C Complete.

Remember: area is the surface covered by a plane shape.

1. L = 8 cm   W = 4 cm   A = _____
2. L = 7 m   W = 3 m   A = _____
3. L = 9 m   W = 6 m   A = _____
4. L = 7 m   W = 4 cm   A = _____
5. L = _____   W = 4 m   A = 24 m^2
6. L = _____   W = 6 cm   A = 36 cm^2
7. L = 15 mm   W = _____   A = 30 mm^2
8. L = 9 cm   W = _____   A = 81 cm^2
9. L = _____   W = 6 m   A = 48 m^2
10. L = 12 m   W = 12 m   A = _____

Score

D Complete.

1. L = 20 cm   W = 5 cm   A = _____
2. L = _____   W = 40 cm   A = 2400 cm^2
3. L = 30 m   W = _____   A = 450 m^2
4. L = 80 cm   W = 30 cm   A = _____
5. L = _____   W = 10 cm   A = 200 cm^2
6. L = 12 m   W = _____   A = 108 m^2
7. L = 15 mm   W = 10 mm   A = _____
8. L = 6 m   W = 1.5 m   A = _____
9. L = 10 m   W = _____   A = 25 m^2
10. L = 100 cm   W = _____   A = 5 m^2

Score

Listen and Write

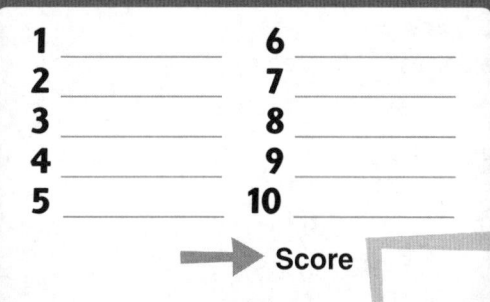

1. _____   6. _____
2. _____   7. _____
3. _____   8. _____
4. _____   9. _____
5. _____   10. _____

Score

Think About It!

a. Whose paddock needs the most fencing? _____

b. Whose paddock has the largest area to cover with SuperPhos? _____

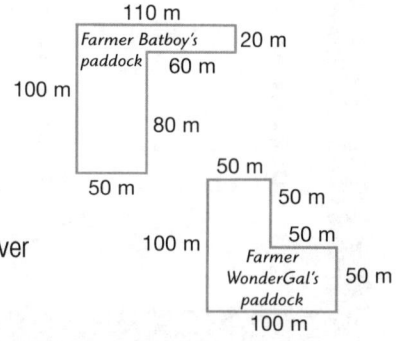

Farmer Batboy's paddock: 110 m, 20 m, 60 m, 80 m, 100 m, 50 m

Farmer WonderGal's paddock: 50 m, 50 m, 50 m, 50 m, 100 m, 100 m

Learning objectives

- Understand and use the formula for the area of a rectangle.
- Understand and calculate perimeters of rectangles.

UNIT 38 Fractions, Decimals, Percentages

Strategies
- ask, 'Does my answer make sense?'
- to multiply a proper fraction by a whole number:
  numerator × whole number ÷ denominator

Remember: in a proper fraction the denominator (bottom number) is greater than the numerator (top number).

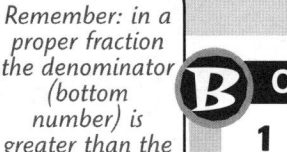

Remember: in an improper fraction the denominator is less than the numerator.

A Complete.
1. As a mixed number? $\frac{9}{5}$ = ___
2. As an improper fraction? $1\frac{2}{5}$ = ___
3. $\frac{1}{5}$ of 15 = ___
4. 3.5 + 1.25 = ___
5. As a decimal? $\frac{3}{10}$ = ___
6. As a fraction? 0.7 = ___
7. 7 − 2.3 = ___
8. $\frac{4}{10}$ of 50 = ___
9. As a fraction? 76% = ___
10. $\frac{15}{100}$ = ___ %

→ Score

B Complete.
1. As a mixed number? $\frac{17}{6}$ = ___
2. As an improper fraction? $2\frac{4}{5}$ = ___
3. $\frac{1}{6}$ of 36 = ___
4. 6.75 + 2.5 = ___
5. As a decimal? $\frac{1}{5}$ = ___
6. As a fraction? 0.3 = ___
7. 0.7 − 0.4 = ___
8. 8 × 0.7 = ___
9. $\frac{7}{10}$ = ___ %
10. As a fraction? 20% = ___

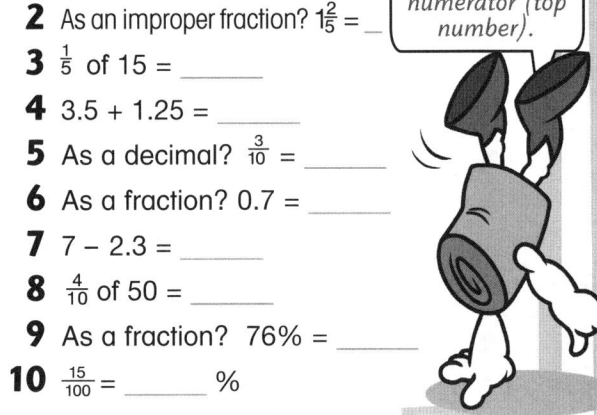

→ Score

Remember: a mixed number is a whole number and a proper fraction.

Remember: a decimal point separates a whole number from the fractional part.

C Complete.
1. As a mixed number? $\frac{23}{4}$ = ___
2. As an improper fraction? $3\frac{1}{5}$ = ___
3. $\frac{2}{3}$ × 12 = ___
4. 3.05 + 3.5 = ___
5. As a decimal? $3\frac{7}{10}$ = ___
6. As a fraction? 0.75 = ___
7. 8.2 − 4.9 = ___
8. 6 × 2.4 = ___
9. $\frac{3}{4}$ = ___ %
10. As a fraction? 18% = ___

→ Score

D Complete.
1. As a mixed number? $\frac{26}{6}$ = ___
2. As an improper fraction? $5\frac{1}{8}$ = ___
3. $\frac{3}{5}$ of 35 = ___
4. 1.01 + 1.11 = ___
5. As a decimal? $6\frac{3}{5}$ = ___
6. As a fraction? 7.35 = ___
7. 7.75 − 1.5 = ___
8. 10 × 9.75 = ___
9. $\frac{3}{5}$ = ___ %
10. As a fraction? 120% = ___

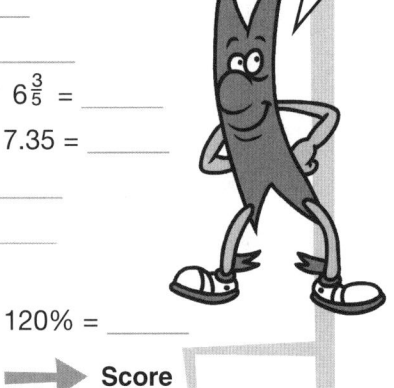

→ Score

Listen and Write
1. ___ 6. ___
2. ___ 7. ___
3. ___ 8. ___
4. ___ 9. ___
5. ___ 10. ___

→ Score

Think About It!
Write in order of size: smallest to largest.

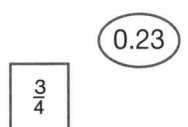

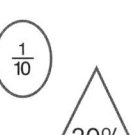

$\frac{3}{4}$ 0.23   25% $\frac{1}{10}$ 30% $\frac{3}{5}$ 0.5

Learning objectives
- Change an improper fraction to a mixed number.
- Relate fractions to division and use division to find simple fractions.
- Use known number facts and place value for mental addition and subtraction.
- Relate fractions to decimal and percentage representation.

Unit 39 Measurement

Strategies
- make all units of measurement the same
- estimate an answer and then ask, 'Does my estimate make sense?'
- use your knowledge of basic number facts

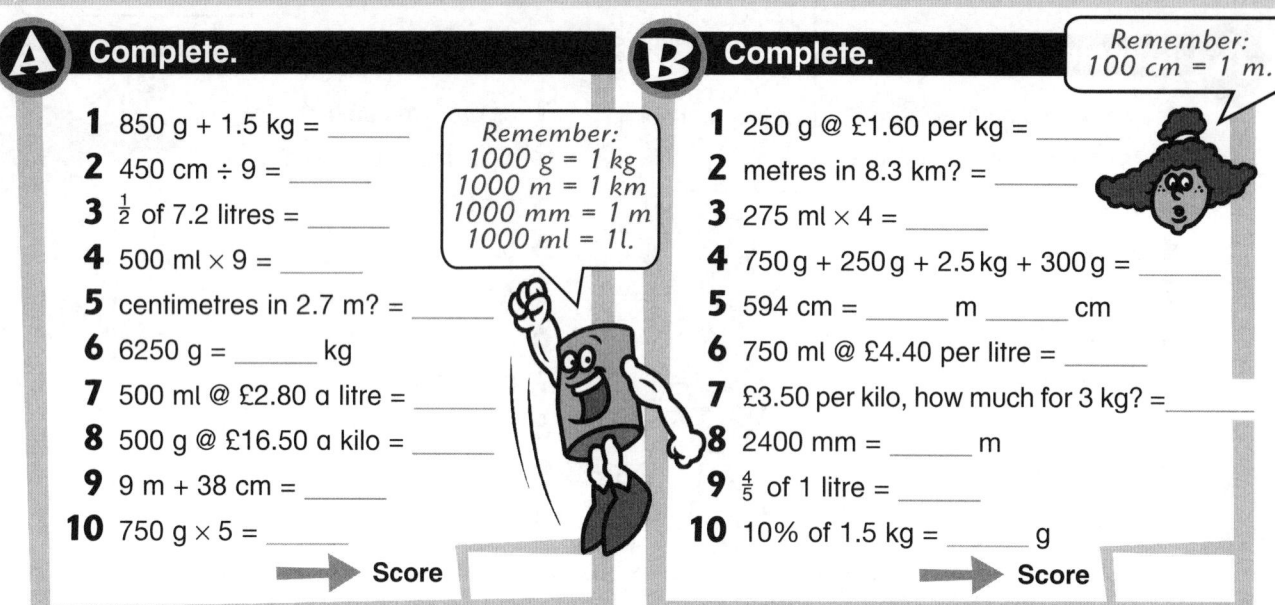

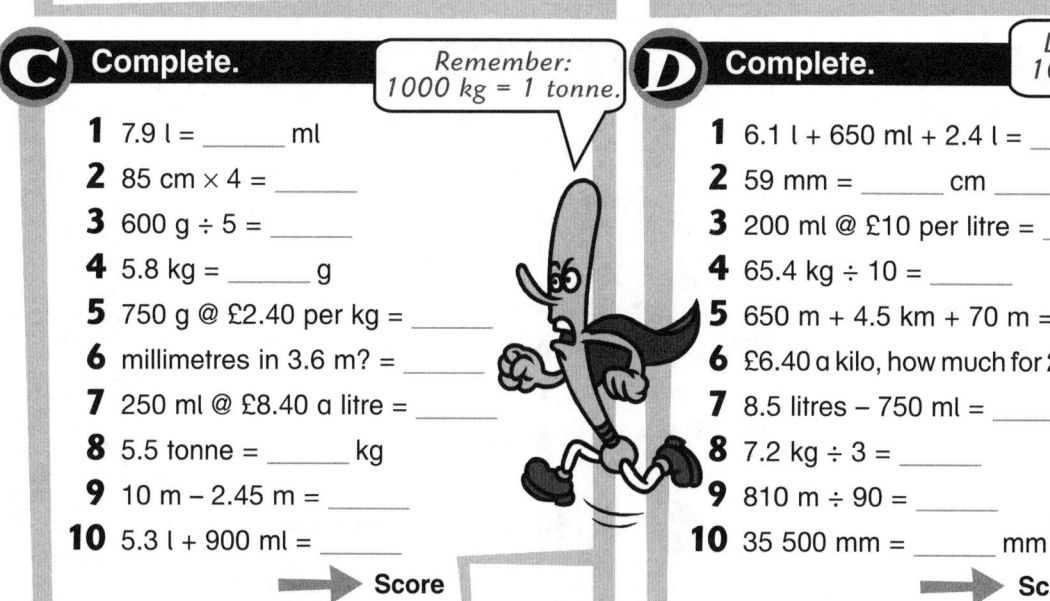

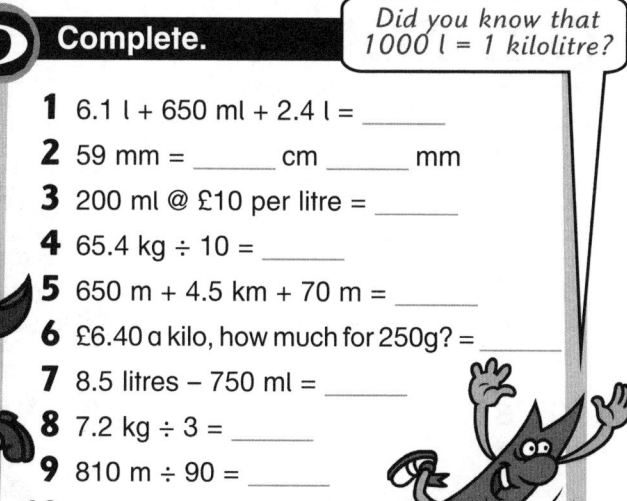

A Complete.

1. 850 g + 1.5 kg = _____
2. 450 cm ÷ 9 = _____
3. $\frac{1}{2}$ of 7.2 litres = _____
4. 500 ml × 9 = _____
5. centimetres in 2.7 m? = _____
6. 6250 g = _____ kg
7. 500 ml @ £2.80 a litre = _____
8. 500 g @ £16.50 a kilo = _____
9. 9 m + 38 cm = _____
10. 750 g × 5 = _____

Score

Remember:
1000 g = 1 kg
1000 m = 1 km
1000 mm = 1 m
1000 ml = 1 l.

B Complete.

1. 250 g @ £1.60 per kg = _____
2. metres in 8.3 km? = _____
3. 275 ml × 4 = _____
4. 750 g + 250 g + 2.5 kg + 300 g = _____
5. 594 cm = _____ m _____ cm
6. 750 ml @ £4.40 per litre = _____
7. £3.50 per kilo, how much for 3 kg? = _____
8. 2400 mm = _____ m
9. $\frac{4}{5}$ of 1 litre = _____
10. 10% of 1.5 kg = _____ g

Score

Remember: 100 cm = 1 m.

C Complete.

1. 7.9 l = _____ ml
2. 85 cm × 4 = _____
3. 600 g ÷ 5 = _____
4. 5.8 kg = _____ g
5. 750 g @ £2.40 per kg = _____
6. millimetres in 3.6 m? = _____
7. 250 ml @ £8.40 a litre = _____
8. 5.5 tonne = _____ kg
9. 10 m – 2.45 m = _____
10. 5.3 l + 900 ml = _____

Score

Remember: 1000 kg = 1 tonne.

D Complete.

1. 6.1 l + 650 ml + 2.4 l = _____
2. 59 mm = _____ cm _____ mm
3. 200 ml @ £10 per litre = _____
4. 65.4 kg ÷ 10 = _____
5. 650 m + 4.5 km + 70 m = _____
6. £6.40 a kilo, how much for 250g? = _____
7. 8.5 litres – 750 ml = _____
8. 7.2 kg ÷ 3 = _____
9. 810 m ÷ 90 = _____
10. 35 500 mm = _____ mm

Score

Did you know that 1000 l = 1 kilolitre?

Listen and Write

1. _____   6. _____
2. _____   7. _____
3. _____   8. _____
4. _____   9. _____
5. _____   10. _____

Score

Think About It!

1. SoupaGuy drinks 300 cartons of milk each day. If each carton contains 600 ml, how many litres does SoupaGuy drink each day?

2. Batboy can lift fifty 2.5 kg weights with one hand and one hundred 250 g weights with the other. How many kilograms can Batboy lift altogether?

Learning objectives
- Solve problems involving measures.
- Convert larger to smaller units.

UNIT 40 Terms

Strategies
- use basic number facts knowledge
- visualise symbols for words (e.g. minus = – quotient = ÷)

Remember: + add; sum of; plus; more than.

Remember: – take away; subtract; minus; less than; difference between.

A Complete.

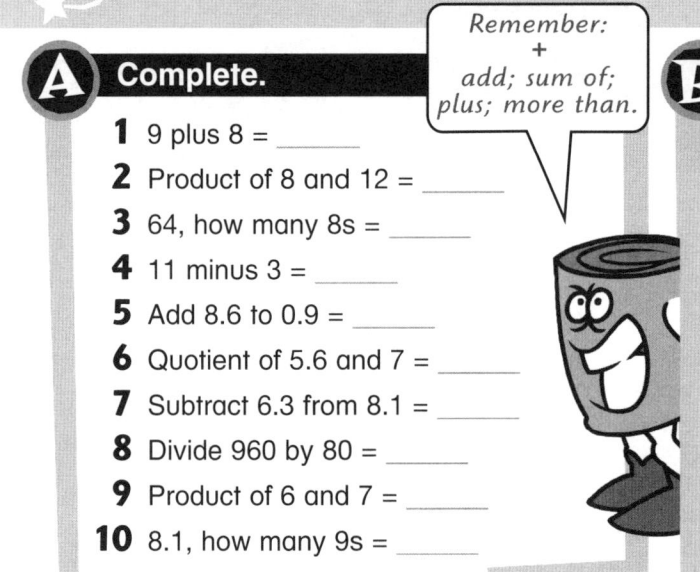

1. 9 plus 8 = _____
2. Product of 8 and 12 = _____
3. 64, how many 8s = _____
4. 11 minus 3 = _____
5. Add 8.6 to 0.9 = _____
6. Quotient of 5.6 and 7 = _____
7. Subtract 6.3 from 8.1 = _____
8. Divide 960 by 80 = _____
9. Product of 6 and 7 = _____
10. 8.1, how many 9s = _____

→ Score ____

B Complete.

1. Add 6.4 and 7.9 = _____
2. Share 80 between 5 = _____
3. Product of 9 and 12 = _____
4. 72 minus 3 eights = _____
5. Quotient of 6300 and 70 = _____
6. Subtract £1.56 from £10 = _____
7. Area of square with sides 6 cm = _____
8. Sum of 5 times 7 and 10 minus 6 = _____
9. Double 847 = _____
10. £58 plus £135 = _____

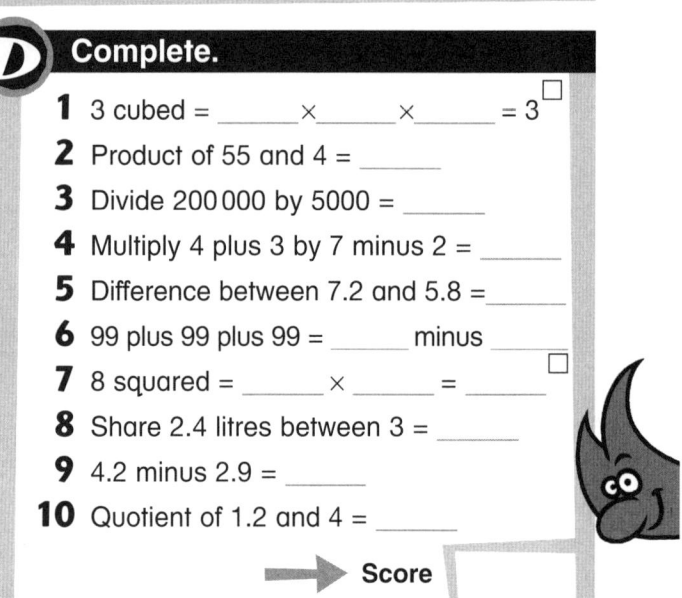

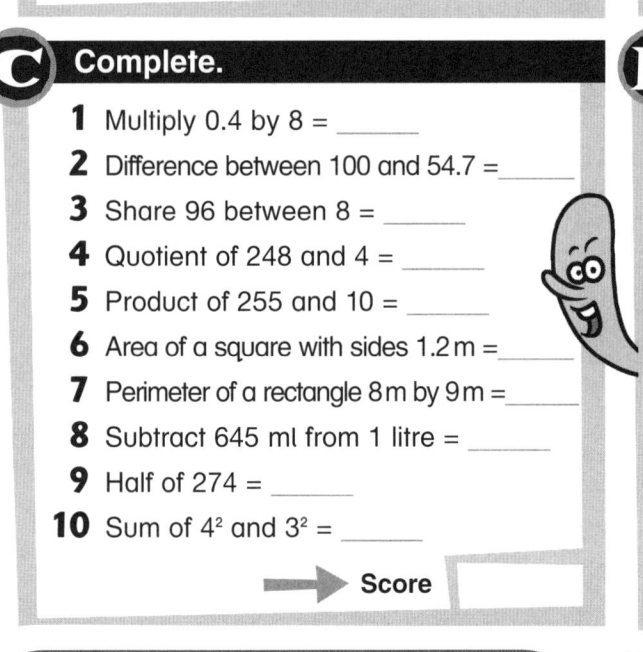

→ Score ____

C Complete.

1. Multiply 0.4 by 8 = _____
2. Difference between 100 and 54.7 = _____
3. Share 96 between 8 = _____
4. Quotient of 248 and 4 = _____
5. Product of 255 and 10 = _____
6. Area of a square with sides 1.2 m = _____
7. Perimeter of a rectangle 8 m by 9 m = _____
8. Subtract 645 ml from 1 litre = _____
9. Half of 274 = _____
10. Sum of 4^2 and 3^2 = _____

→ Score ____

D Complete.

1. 3 cubed = _____ × _____ × _____ = $3^{□}$
2. Product of 55 and 4 = _____
3. Divide 200 000 by 5000 = _____
4. Multiply 4 plus 3 by 7 minus 2 = _____
5. Difference between 7.2 and 5.8 = _____
6. 99 plus 99 plus 99 = _____ minus _____$^{□}$
7. 8 squared = _____ × _____ = _____
8. Share 2.4 litres between 3 = _____
9. 4.2 minus 2.9 = _____
10. Quotient of 1.2 and 4 = _____

→ Score ____

Listen and Write

1 _____   6 _____
2 _____   7 _____
3 _____   8 _____
4 _____   9 _____
5 _____ 10 _____

→ Score ____

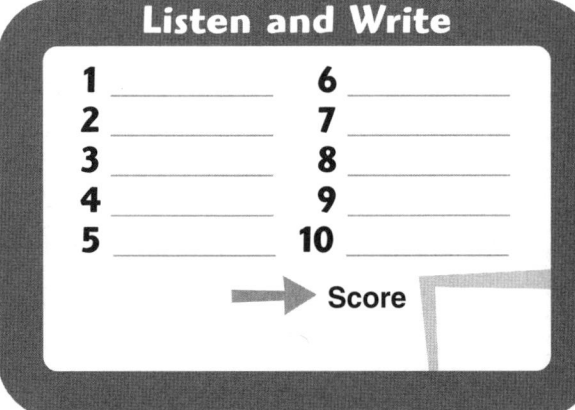

Think About It!

Match all the terms that mean the same by making them the same colour.

multiply | sum of | squared | share | – | ÷ | times | + | difference | minus | × | product | quotient | less | add | plus | divide

Learning objective
- Understand and use mathematical vocabulary.

63

© OUP: Copying permitted for purchasing school only.

Review 8

A Complete.
1. 7 + 6 = _____
2. 4 × 8 = _____
3. 35 ÷ 7 = _____
4. 16 − 9 = _____
5. Perimeter of a square with sides 8 cm = _____
6. $\frac{3}{4} - \frac{1}{8}$ = _____
7. 7455 g = _____ kg
8. 1500 mm @ £60 per metre = _____
9. As a decimal? $\frac{1}{5}$ = _____
10. Product of 6 and 0.7 = _____

→ Score

B Complete.
1. _____ + 8 = 12
2. 7 × _____ = 56
3. _____ ÷ 3 = 18
4. 15 − _____ = 8
5. Area of a square with sides 9 m = _____
6. $\frac{1}{8}$ of 64 = _____
7. 250 ml @ £3.60 a litre = _____
8. 72.8 kg ÷ 4 = _____
9. As a fraction? 1.6 = _____
10. Quotient of 28.8 and 4 = _____

→ Score

C Complete.
1. 5 + _____ = 14
2. _____ × 6 = 36
3. 54 ÷ _____ = 9
4. _____ − 4 = 9
5. L = 6 m W = 4 m so P = _____ and A = _____
6. $\frac{7}{8} + \frac{3}{4}$ = _____
7. 885 mm = _____ cm _____ mm
8. £4.80 a kilo, how much for 750 g? = _____
9. $\frac{5}{20}$ = _____ %
10. Sum of $\frac{5}{8}$ and $\frac{1}{16}$ = _____

→ Score

D Complete.
1. 12 + 12 = _____
2. 33 = 3 × _____
3. 7 = _____ + 6
4. 14 − 9 = _____
5. L = 20 cm W = 4 cm so P = _____ and A = _____
6. $\frac{3}{4}$ of 48 = _____
7. millimetres in 7.4 metres? = _____
8. 5.2 l − 975 ml = _____
9. 10 × 5.75 = _____
10. Difference between 9.4 and 3.7 = _____

→ Score

Listen and Write
1. _____   6. _____
2. _____   7. _____
3. _____   8. _____
4. _____   9. _____
5. _____   10. _____

→ Score

Think About It!

Identify these two numbers.
- We have a sum of 17.
- We have a difference of 7.
- We have a product of 60 and a quotient of 2.4.

We are… _____ and _____

Check-up
- I can recognise equivalence between fractions and decimals.
- I can find the area and perimeter of rectangles from given dimensions.
- I can convert smaller to larger metric units and vice versa.

Take a Break 8

To get to his spaceship Rick Rocket must take a path through the Marsh on Mars.

Only one path is correct and Rick can only move horizontally or vertically one square at a time.

$8^2 = 8 + 8$	$8^2 = 8 - 8$	$8^2 = 64$	$8^2 = 8 \div 8$	$8^2 = 64 \div 8$	$8^2 = 88$
$\frac{1}{4}$ of 24 = 12	$\frac{1}{4}$ of 24 = 4	$\frac{1}{4}$ of 24 = 6	$\frac{1}{4}$ of 24 = 8	$\frac{1}{4}$ of 24 = 2	$\frac{1}{4}$ of 24 = 3
$9 + 7 = 16$	$9 \times 7 = 7 \times 9$	$9 \times 7 = 63$	$9 \times 7 = 79$	$9 + 7 = 2$	$9 + 7 = 97$
$4^2 = 16$	$4 \times 4 = 8$	$4^2 = 8$	$4 \times 4 = 16$	$4 + 4 = 8$	$4 \times 4 = 4$
$24 \div 3 = 8$	$24 \div 3 = 12$	$24 \div 3 = 6$	$24 \div 3 = 9$	$24 \div 3 = 3 \times 24$	$24 \div 3 = 2^2$
$6 \times 8 = 48$	$8 \times 6 = 48$	$48 \div 6 = 8$	$7^2 - 1 = 48$	$24 \times 2 = 48$	$12 \times 4 = 48$
$12 \times 3 = 123$	$3 \times 12 = 312$	$12 \times 3 = 15$	$3 \times 12 = 24$	$12 \times 3 = 18$	$3 \times 12 = 36$
$\frac{1}{3}$ of 12 = 3	$27 \div 9 = 3$	$\frac{1}{4}$ of 12 = 3	$\frac{1}{3}$ of 9 = 3	$3^2 - 2 \times 3 = 3$	$9 \div 3 = 3$
$4 \times 6 = 42$	$6 \times 4 = 24$	$6 \times 4 = 20$	$24 \div 4 = 4$	$24 \div 6 = 6$	$\frac{1}{4}$ of 24 = 4
$9^2 = 18$	$9^2 = 81$	$9^2 = 99$	$9^2 = 9 + 9$	$9^2 = 9 \times 9$	$9^2 = 9 \div 9$

Learning objectives
- Know by heart multiplication facts up to 10 × 10 and derive quickly corresponding division facts.
- Relate fractions to division and use division to find simple fractions.
- Know squares of numbers to at least 10 × 10.

© OUP: Copying permitted for purchasing school only.

Important Facts

Tables

0 × 2 = 0	0 × 3 = 0	0 × 4 = 0	0 × 5 = 0	0 × 6 = 0
1 × 2 = 2	1 × 3 = 3	1 × 4 = 4	1 × 5 = 5	1 × 6 = 6
2 × 2 = 4	2 × 3 = 6	2 × 4 = 8	2 × 5 = 10	2 × 6 = 12
3 × 2 = 6	3 × 3 = 9	3 × 4 = 12	3 × 5 = 15	3 × 6 = 18
4 × 2 = 8	4 × 3 = 12	4 × 4 = 16	4 × 5 = 20	4 × 6 = 24
5 × 2 = 10	5 × 3 = 15	5 × 4 = 20	5 × 5 = 25	5 × 6 = 30
6 × 2 = 12	6 × 3 = 18	6 × 4 = 24	6 × 5 = 30	6 × 6 = 36
7 × 2 = 14	7 × 3 = 21	7 × 4 = 28	7 × 5 = 35	7 × 6 = 42
8 × 2 = 16	8 × 3 = 24	8 × 4 = 32	8 × 5 = 40	8 × 6 = 48
9 × 2 = 18	9 × 3 = 27	9 × 4 = 36	9 × 5 = 45	9 × 6 = 54
10 × 2 = 20	10 × 3 = 30	10 × 4 = 40	10 × 5 = 50	10 × 6 = 60

0 × 7 = 0	0 × 8 = 0	0 × 9 = 0	0 × 10 = 0
1 × 7 = 7	1 × 8 = 8	1 × 9 = 9	1 × 10 = 10
2 × 7 = 14	2 × 8 = 16	2 × 9 = 18	2 × 10 = 20
3 × 7 = 21	3 × 8 = 24	3 × 9 = 27	3 × 10 = 30
4 × 7 = 28	4 × 8 = 32	4 × 9 = 36	4 × 10 = 40
5 × 7 = 35	5 × 8 = 40	5 × 9 = 45	5 × 10 = 50
6 × 7 = 42	6 × 8 = 48	6 × 9 = 54	6 × 10 = 60
7 × 7 = 49	7 × 8 = 56	7 × 9 = 63	7 × 10 = 70
8 × 7 = 56	8 × 8 = 64	8 × 9 = 72	8 × 10 = 80
9 × 7 = 63	9 × 8 = 72	9 × 9 = 81	9 × 10 = 90
10 × 7 = 70	10 × 8 = 80	10 × 9 = 90	10 × 10 = 100

Prime numbers

2, 3, 5, 7, 11, 13, 17, 19, 23, 29, 31, 37, 41, 43, 47, 53, 59, 61, 67, 71, 73, 79, 83, 89, 97

Square numbers

$1^2 = 1$
$2^2 = 4$
$3^2 = 9$
$4^2 = 16$
$5^2 = 25$
$6^2 = 36$
$7^2 = 49$
$8^2 = 64$
$9^2 = 81$
$10^2 = 100$
$11^2 = 121$
$12^2 = 144$
$13^2 = 169$
$14^2 = 196$
$15^2 = 225$
$20^2 = 400$
$100^2 = 10\,000$

Measurement

Length: 10 millimetres (mm) = 1 centimetre (cm)
100 centimetres = 1 metre (m)
1000 metres = 1 kilometre (km)

Mass: 1000 grams (g) = 1 kilogram (kg)
1000 kilograms = 1 tonne

Capacity: 1000 millilitres (ml) = 1 litre (l)

Area: 10 000 square metres (m^2) = 1 hectare (ha)

Money: 100 pence (p) = 1 pound (£)
@ means at the cost of

Time

60 seconds = 1 minute
60 minutes = 1 hour
24 hours = 1 day
7 days = 1 week
2 weeks = 1 fortnight
12 months = 1 year
13 months = 1 lunar year
10 years = 1 decade
100 years = 1 century
1000 years = 1 millennium

Seasons

Spring: March, April, May
Summer: June, July, August
Autumn: September, October, November
Winter: December, January, February

The Order of Operations

Do **brackets** first followed by **of** then **multiplication** and **division** in the order they appear from left to right, and finally **addition** and **subtraction** in the order they appear from left to right.

Addition

odd + odd = even
even + even = even
odd + even = odd
even + odd = odd

Subtraction

odd − odd = even
even − even = even
odd − even = odd
even − odd = odd

Class Record Sheet

Pupil's Progress Chart

Name: _____

Unit	Date	Classroom score				Homework score				Signed	Comments
		A	B	C	D	A	B	C	D		
1											
2											
3											
4											
5											
REVIEW 1											
6											
7											
8											
9											
10											
REVIEW 2											
11											
12											
13											
14											
15											
REVIEW 3											
16											
17											
18											
19											
20											
REVIEW 4											

© OUP: Copying permitted for purchasing school only.

Pupil's Progress Chart

Name: _____

Unit	Date	Classroom score				Homework score				Signed	Comments
		A	B	C	D	A	B	C	D		
21											
22											
23											
24											
25											
REVIEW 5											
26											
27											
28											
29											
30											
REVIEW 6											
31											
32											
33											
34											
35											
REVIEW 7											
36											
37											
38											
39											
40											
REVIEW 8											

© OUP: Copying permitted for purchasing school only.

Listen and Write

Teacher's Questions with Answers

Unit 1 Number Facts
1. Add 4 to 9 (13)
2. Subtract 6 from 9 (3)
3. Multiply 3 by 3 (9)
4. Divide 45 by 9 (5)
5. 7×3 (21)
6. $8 + 5$ (13)
7. $16 - 7$ (9)
8. 5^2 (25)
9. $24 \div 4$ (6)
10. 5×4 (20)

Unit 2 Extended Number Facts
1. $16 + 8$ (24)
2. $36 + 8$ (44)
3. $66 + 8$ (74)
4. $360 + 80$ (440)
5. $12 - 5$ (7)
6. $42 - 5$ (37)
7. $420 - 50$ (370)
8. 40×30 (1200)
9. $240 \div 6$ (40)
10. $? \times 30 = 900$ (30)

Unit 3 Counting & Order
What comes next?
1. 20 40 60 80 ? (100)
2. 33 30 27 24 ? (21)
3. 5 10 15 20 ? (25)
4. 70 120 170 220 ? (270)
5. 0.3 0.4 0.5 0.6 ? (0.7)
6. £25 £32 £39 £46 ? (£53)
7. 823 1123 1423 1723 ? (2023)
8. 1230 1130 1030 930 ? (830)
9. 10.3 10.6 10.9 11.2 ? (11.5)
10. 144 121 100 81 ? (64)

Unit 4 Length
1. cm in 1 metre (100)
2. 1 metre – 35 cm (65 cm)
3. 200 cm $\div$ 10 (20 cm)
4. $\frac{1}{2}$ of 1 km (500 m)
5. 1 km + 350 m (1.35 km or 1350 m)
6. cm in 1.5 m? (150)
7. 7 cm + 5 mm = ? mm (75 mm)
8. 40 km $\div$ 5 (8 km)
9. 1 metre – 250 mm (750 mm or 0.75 m)
10. millimetres in 1.2 m (1200 mm)

Unit 5 Place Value
1. $70 + 8000 + 400 + 2$ (8472)
2. $6 + 5000$ (5006)
3. Value of 8 in 3894? (800)
4. 100 less than 937 (837)
5. 125.6 = 12 tens + 5 units + ? tenths (6)
6. 14 hundreds 32 units (1432)
7. Value of 7 in 346.75? (7 tenths)
8. Value of 3 in 21.03? (3 hundredths)
9. 53 564 = 533 hundred + ? units (64 units)
10. $10 + 1 + 10000$ (10 011)

REVIEW 1
1. 6×5 (30)
2. Value of 4 in 3451? (400)
3. Next? 6 12 18 24 ? (30)
4. Value of 3 in 73.55? (3 units)
5. 1 km – 750 m (250 m)
6. Divide 240 by 3 (80)
7. $8 + 7 + 9$ (24)
8. Subtract 6 from 23 (7)
9. 1 m + 5 cm + 5 mm (1.055 m or 1055 mm)
10. $30\,000 + 3 + 3000 + 300$ (33 303)

Unit 6 Number Facts
1. $7 + 9$ (16)
2. 5×9 (45)
3. 14 minus 8 (6)
4. 7×4 (28)
5. 5 @ £4 each (£20)
6. Divide 32 by 8 (4)
7. 9×7 (63)
8. 8^2 (64)
9. $54 \div 6$ (9)
10. Subtract 9 from 16 (7)

Unit 7 Money
1. £1 – 20p (80p)
2. £10 – £5.50 (£4.50)
3. 9 @ £5 each (£45)
4. £1.40, how many 20 pence coins? (7)
5. £3.60 $\div$ 6 (60p)
6. 500 g @ £1.20 per kilo (60p)
7. Pence in £9.40 (940)
8. Change from £5 if I spend £3.75? (£1.25)
9. 7 pens @ £1.50 each (£10.50)
10. £4, how many 10 pence coins? (40)

Unit 8 Fractions
1. $\frac{1}{2}$ of 16 (8)
2. $\frac{1}{4}$ of 12 (3)
3. $\frac{1}{4}$ of 20 (5)
4. 6 lots of $\frac{1}{2}$ (3)
5. 8 lots of $\frac{1}{4}$ (2)
6. $\frac{3}{4}$ of 24 (18)
7. $1 - \frac{1}{2}$ ($\frac{1}{2}$)
8. $\frac{7}{8} - \frac{4}{8}$ ($\frac{3}{8}$)
9. $\frac{5}{6} - \frac{1}{6}$ ($\frac{4}{6}$)
10. $2\frac{1}{2} - 1\frac{1}{4}$ ($1\frac{1}{4}$)

Unit 9 Decimals
1. As a decimal $\frac{1}{10}$ (0.1)
2. As a fraction 0.5 ($\frac{5}{10}$ or $\frac{1}{2}$)
3. As a fraction 0.9 ($\frac{9}{10}$)
4. As a decimal $\frac{1}{4}$ (0.25)
5. As a decimal $1\frac{7}{10}$ (1.7)
6. As a fraction 3.5 ($3\frac{1}{2}$)
7. $3.8 + 1.2$ (5)
8. $2.3 - 0.9$ (1.4)
9. $1.6 + 0.2$ (1.8)
10. $3.1 - 0.7$ (2.4)

Unit 10 Equations
1. $(2 + 5) \times (7 - 4)$ (21)
2. $24 - ? = 18$ (6)
3. $20 \div 5 + 8$ (12)
4. $\frac{1}{2}$ of $10 \times \frac{1}{2}$ of 12 (30)
5. $(1.2 + 0.8) \times 8$ (16)
6. $4 \times 6 \div 3$ (8)
7. $48 \times 5 = 24 \times ?$ (10)
8. $56 \div (21 \div 3)$ (8)
9. $6 \times 15 = 3 \times ?$ (30)
10. $20 - 6 \times 3 + 7$ (9)

REVIEW 2
1. $\frac{1}{2}$ of 72 (36)
2. 8×9 (72)
3. $54 \div 9$ (6)
4. $\frac{1}{4}$ of 24×5 (30)
5. As a decimal $2\frac{3}{10}$ (2.3)
6. $\frac{2}{3}$ of 24 (16)
7. As a fraction 0.8 ($\frac{8}{10}$ or $\frac{4}{5}$)
8. $8 \times (24 \div 6)$ (32)
9. Subtract 4 from the sum of 8 and 9 (13)
10. $2.1 - 0.6$ (1.5)

Unit 11 Number Facts
1. 40 ÷ 5 (8)
2. Subtract 7 from 16 (9)
3. Multiply 6 by 7 (42)
4. Sum of 9, 6 and 7 (22)
5. 11 + 9 (20)
6. Divide 28 by 4 (7)
7. 10^2 (100)
8. 7 × 7 (49)
9. 7 + 8 (15)
10. 8 × 0 (0)

Unit 12 Time
1. 2 hours = ? minutes (120)
2. $\frac{3}{4}$ of 1 hour = ? minutes (45)
3. 60 km in 3 hours = ? km/h (20)
4. 3 days = ? hours (72)
5. Days in April and May? (61)
6. How long from 8:30 a.m. to 9:20 a.m.? (50 mins)
7. 60 km/h for $2\frac{1}{2}$ hrs (150 km)
8. 6:10 p.m. − 20 minutes (5:50 p.m.)
9. $\frac{1}{5}$ of 1 hour (12 mins)
10. How many seconds in $3\frac{1}{2}$ minutes? (210 secs)

Unit 13 Fractions & Decimals
1. $\frac{3}{8} + \frac{1}{8}$ ($\frac{1}{2}$ or $\frac{4}{8}$)
2. As a decimal $\frac{3}{5}$ (0.6)
3. 1.5 − 0.9 (0.6)
4. $\frac{2}{3}$ of 12 (8)
5. $\frac{7}{10}$ of 30 (21)
6. $\frac{8}{10} - \frac{1}{10}$ ($\frac{7}{10}$)
7. As a decimal $2\frac{1}{2}$ (2.5)
8. As a fraction 7.25 ($7\frac{1}{4}$)
9. $\frac{3}{8}$ of 24 (9)
10. 6.4 ÷ 10 (0.64)

Unit 14 Place Value
1. 4000 + 400 + 40 + 4 (4444)
2. Value of 1 in 743 127? (100)
3. 9.1 = 9 units + ? (1 tenth)
4. 1 + 10 000 + 100 (10 101)
5. 50 hundreds + 50 (5050)
6. 1000 more than 81 234? (82 234)
7. 6 units + $\frac{24}{100}$ + 70 (76.24)
8. Value of 3 in 264.31? ($\frac{3}{10}$)
9. 1 million less than 83 096 540 (82 096 540)
10. Value of 4 in 0.14? ($\frac{4}{100}$)

Unit 15 Doubling & Halving
1. 2 × 410 (820)
2. Half of 450 (225)
3. Double 37 (74)
4. $\frac{1}{2}$ of 184 (92)
5. 348 × 2 (696)
6. $\frac{1}{2}$ of 1640 (820)
7. Their score was 394. Our score was double theirs. What was our score? (768)
8. 248 ÷ 2 (124)
9. I had 58 but lost half. How many now? (29)
10. Double 3064 (6128)

REVIEW 3
1. 14 − 9 (5)
2. Value of 3 in 18.63? ($\frac{3}{100}$)
3. Minutes in 4 hrs? (240)
4. 9 × 7 (63)
5. 40 km/h for 3 hours (120 km)
6. Sum of 1.6 and 0.7 (2.3)
7. 11:15 a.m. + $4\frac{1}{2}$ hours (3:45 p.m.)
8. $\frac{7}{8}$ × 56 (49)
9. Value of 24 in 124 359 (24 000)
10. $\frac{7}{10} - \frac{2}{5}$ ($\frac{3}{10}$)

Unit 16 Number Facts
1. 9 + 5 + 7 (21)
2. 81 ÷ ? = 9 (9)
3. 13 − 7 (6)
4. Multiply 8 by 6 (48)
5. 6 @ £9 each (£54)
6. 6^2 (36)
7. 27 ÷ 3 (9)
8. 4 × 8 (32)
9. 0 × 7 (0)
10. ? × 7 = 35 (5)

Unit 17 Equations
1. ($\frac{1}{2}$ of 20) × 5 (50)
2. 7 × (4 + 2) (42)
3. (3 × 8) + (12 ÷ 3) (28)
4. $\frac{1}{4}$ × 8 × $\frac{1}{3}$ of 18 (12)
5. (11 − 4) + (4 × 3) (19)
6. 5 × 9 − 4 × 5 (25)
7. (£50 − £35) + (£50 − £15) (£50)
8. 36 × 5 = 18 × ? (10)
9. 4 × ($\frac{1}{3}$ of 24) (32)
10. (12 ÷ 2) × (5 − 2) (28)

Unit 18 Mass
1. 500 g + 375 g (875 g)
2. 400 g × 5 (2 kg or 2000 g)
3. $\frac{1}{4}$ of 1 kg (250 g)
4. 5.7 kg + 600 g (6.3 kg)
5. 0.5 of 1 kg (500 g)
6. 500 g @ £4.20 a kilo? (£2.10)
7. Hector has a mass of 32.5 kg. Victor has a mass of 45.7 kg. What is their total mass? (78.2 kg)
8. 250 g @ £16 a kilo (£4)
9. 53.5 kg × 10 (535 kg)
10. $\frac{1}{4}$ of 2.4 kg (600 g)

Unit 19 Percentages
1. As a percentage $\frac{50}{100}$ (50%)
2. As a fraction 25% ($\frac{1}{4}$)
3. As a decimal 60% (0.6)
4. As a percentage $\frac{1}{2}$ (50%)
5. As a decimal 40% (0.4)
6. As a fraction 75% ($\frac{3}{4}$ or $\frac{75}{100}$)
7. As a percentage $\frac{20}{50}$ (40%)
8. As a fraction 91% ($\frac{91}{100}$)
9. As a percentage $\frac{10}{25}$ (40%)
10. As a decimal 63% (0.63)

Unit 20 Counting & Order
What comes next?
1. 43 45 49 ? (51)
2. 7 14 21 28 ? (35)
3. $\frac{1}{4}$ $\frac{1}{2}$ $\frac{3}{4}$ $1\frac{1}{4}$? ($1\frac{1}{2}$)
4. 114 789 115 789 116 789 117 789 ? (118 789)
5. 0.2 0.7 1.2 1.7 ? (2.2)
6. 3 6 12 24 ? (48)
7. 86 79 72 65 ? (58)
8. 2337 1837 1337 837 ? (337)
9. £5.25 £5.50 £5.75 £6 ? (£6.25)
10. 448 224 112 66 ? (33)

REVIEW 4
1. 8 × 5 (40)
2. 1.4 − 0.7 (0.7)
3. Double 83 (166)
4. $\frac{1}{4}$ of 16 × $\frac{1}{5}$ of 30 (24)
5. As a fraction 90% ($\frac{9}{10}$)
6. As a decimal $\frac{3}{4}$ (0.75)
7. 250 g @ £1.20 per kilo (30p)
8. Next? 83 77 71 65 ? (59)
9. As a percentage $\frac{1}{4}$ (25%)
10. 3 × 9 + 8 × 2 (43)

71

Unit 21 Number Facts
1. 4×9 (36)
2. Sum of 8 and 9 (17)
3. Multiply 6 by 7 (42)
4. Divide 100 by 10 (10)
5. 15 minus 6 (9)
6. 8×7 (56)
7. $49 \div 7$ (7)
8. 6^2 (36)
9. 8 @ 5p each (40p)
10. What is the difference between 14 and 8? (6)

Unit 22 Extended Number Facts
1. $58 + 9$ (67)
2. $580 + 90$ (670)
3. 40×8 (320)
4. 70×30 (210)
5. $13 - 6$ (7)
6. $173 - 6$ (167)
7. $530 - 60$ (470)
8. $480 \div 80$ (6)
9. $480 \div 8$ (60)
10. $1357 + ? = 4357$ (3000)

Unit 23 Capacity
1. 5 l = ? ml (5000)
2. 7×6 l (42 l)
3. 10 l – 500 ml (9.5 l or 9500 ml)
4. 600 ml $\div$ 10 (60 ml)
5. 500 ml @ £2.70 per litre (£1.35)
6. $\frac{1}{4}$ of 2.4 l (600 ml)
7. 250 ml @ £12 a litre (£4)
8. How many 500 ml bottles to fill an 8 l bucket? (16)
9. 1.8 l + 300 ml (2.1 l or 2100 ml)
10. 200 ml $\times$ 8 (1.6 l or 1600 ml)

Unit 24 Equations
1. ($\frac{1}{4}$ of 20) $\times$ ($\frac{1}{3}$ of 18) (30)
2. $9 + (3 \times 6)$ (27)
3. $(9 + 3) \times 6$ (72)
4. ($\frac{2}{5}$ of 25) – 10 (5)
5. $48 \times 4 = ? \times 2$ (96)
6. $100 - (4 \times 6)$ (76)
7. $300 \times (4 + 50) \times (4 + 7) \times 4 = ? \times 4$ (357)
8. $56 \div (15 - 7)$ (7)
9. $(15 \div 5) + 5$ (8)
10. $15 \div (5 + 5)$ (1.5)

Unit 25 Counting & Order
What comes next?
1. 26 36 46 56 ? (66)
2. 53 49 45 41 ? (37)
3. 0.3 0.7 1.1 1.5 ? (1.9)
4. 774 804 834 864 ? (894)
5. $\frac{1}{10}$ $\frac{1}{5}$ $\frac{3}{10}$ $\frac{2}{5}$? ($\frac{1}{2}$ or $\frac{5}{10}$)
6. 18.7 17.6 16.5 15.4 ? (14.3)
7. 72 345 76 345 80 345 84 345 ? (88 345)
8. 5 10 20 40 ? (80)
9. $\frac{1}{6}$ $\frac{5}{6}$ $1\frac{1}{2}$ $2\frac{1}{6}$? ($2\frac{5}{6}$)
10. 12.75 12.25 11.75 11.25 ? (10.75)

REVIEW 5
1. $6 + 9$ (15)
2. 8×7 (56)
3. $48 \div 6$ (8)
4. 250 ml @ £20 per l (£5)
5. Next? 73 103 133 163 ? (193)
6. $8 \times 4 - \frac{1}{4}$ of 36 (23)
7. 45c a litre. How much for 6 litres? (£2.70)
8. Next? 1.2 1.5 1.8 ? (2.1)
9. $(60 - 40) + \frac{1}{7}$ of 35 (4)
10. 6×90 (540)

Unit 26 Number Facts
1. 14 plus 9 (23)
2. 8×5 (40)
3. 15 minus 7 (8)
4. $42 \div 6$ (7)
5. 7 @ £9 each (£63)
6. 9^2 (81)
7. 12×10 (120)
8. Double 78 (156)
9. $17 - 9$ (8)
10. Half of 74 (37)

Unit 27 Money
1. £10 – £2.75 (£7.25)
2. £5, how many 10 pence coins? (50)
3. 8 @ £3.50 each (£28)
4. £9.50, how many 50 pence coins? (19)
5. Change from £20 if I buy 6 @ £1.50? (£11)
6. 500 g @ £6.48 per kilo (£3.24)
7. I had £7.50. I spent £3.25. How much now? (£4.25)
8. 7 @ £4.30 each (£30.10)
9. Change from £50 if I spend £19.50? (£30.50)
10. 5 kg @ £3.25 a kilo (£16.25)

Unit 28 Factors
What is the missing factor?
1. $10 = 5 \times ?$ (2)
2. $12 = 2 \times ?$ (6)
3. $9 = 3 \times ?$ (3)
4. $8 = 4 \times ?$ (2)
5. $20 = 2 \times ?$ (10)
6. $12 = 3 \times ?$ (4)
7. $20 = 5 \times ?$ (4)
8. $24 = 6 \times ?$ (4)
9. $24 = 2 \times 3 \times ?$ (4)
10. $30 = 10 \times ?$ (3)

Unit 29 Fractions & Decimals
1. $\frac{3}{4}$ of 12 (9)
2. $0.3 + 1.8$ (2.1)
3. $\frac{1}{4} + \frac{1}{8}$ ($\frac{3}{8}$)
4. As a decimal 50% (0.5)
5. As a percentage $\frac{1}{4}$ (25%)
6. As a fraction 30% ($\frac{30}{100}$ or $\frac{3}{10}$)
7. $\frac{1}{2} - \frac{1}{8}$ ($\frac{3}{8}$)
8. 0.5×0.5 (0.25)
9. $7 \times \frac{1}{5}$ ($1\frac{2}{5}$ or $\frac{7}{5}$)
10. 10% of £90 (£9)

Unit 30 Place Value
1. $500 + 50\,000 + 7 + 6000 + 80$ (56 587)
2. $40 + 1 + 0.5$ (41.5)
3. Hundreds in 1897 (18)
4. $500 + 4 + \frac{37}{100} + 40$ (544.37)
5. Value of 7 in 1 706 942? (7 hundred thousand)
6. $\frac{1}{100} + 6 + \frac{6}{10} + 10$ (16.61)
7. Value of 3 in 542.013? ($\frac{3}{1000}$)
8. How many tens in 15 000? (1500)
9. 10 000 less than 791 600 (781 600)
10. $80 + \frac{7}{10} + 3000 + 500 + \frac{3}{100} + 3$ (3583.73)

REVIEW 6
1. 6×9 (54)
2. $45 \div 9$ (5)
3. 9 @ £5.50 each (£49.50)
4. $\frac{1}{4} + \frac{3}{8}$ ($\frac{5}{8}$)
5. Value of 1 in 37.017? $\frac{1}{100}$
6. 15 @ 40p each (£6)
7. 1000 more than 875 469 (876 469)
8. Change from £10 if I spend £8.45? (£1.55)
9. 10% of £60 (£6)
10. $\frac{3}{8}$ of £48

Unit 31 Number Facts

1. 8×3 (24)
2. Subtract 9 from 11 (2)
3. $54 \div 9$ (6)
4. Product of 7 and 9 (63)
5. Sum of 8, 7 and 6 (21)
6. Divide 49 by 7 (7)
7. 12^2 (144)
8. 9 @ £8 each (£72)
9. $15 - 8$ (7)
10. 9×4 (36)

Unit 32 Square Numbers

1. 3^2 (9)
2. 7^2 (49)
3. 6^2 (36)
4. 10^2 (100)
5. 2^2 (4)
6. 8^2 (64)
7. 4^2 (16)
8. 9^2 (81)
9. 2^2 (4)
10. $2^2 + 11^2$ (125)

Unit 33 Time

1. $2\frac{3}{4}$ hours = ? mins (165)
2. 25 km @ 10 km/h = ? hours (2.5 hrs or $2\frac{1}{2}$ hrs)
3. 85 seconds = ? mins ? secs (1 min 25 seconds)
4. How many years in $4\frac{1}{2}$ centuries? (450)
5. $2\frac{1}{4}$ hours after midnight (2:15 a.m.)
6. Days in June and July? (61)
7. 9:35 + 45 minutes (10:20)
8. Minutes from 7:55 to 9:15 (80)
9. $7\frac{1}{2}$ decades = ? years (75)
10. 3.5 hours before noon (8:30 a.m.)

Unit 34 Counting & Order

What comes next?

1. 32 37 42 47 ? (52)
2. 1.1 2.2 3.3 4.4 ? (5.5)
3. 75 69 63 57 ? (51)
4. $\frac{3}{16}$ $\frac{5}{16}$ $\frac{7}{16}$ $\frac{9}{16}$? ($\frac{11}{16}$)
5. 45 901 45 501 45 101 44 701 ? (44 301)
6. 32.05 32.08 32.11 32.14 ? (32.17)
7. 9850 9790 9730 9670 ? (9610)
8. 36 49 64 81 ? (100)
9. 30 60 120 240 ? (480)
10. £8.25 £9.75 £11.25 ? (£12.75)

Unit 35 Equations

1. $7 \times 6 \times 5$ (210)
2. $68 \times 9 = 60 \times 9 + ?$ (8×9 or 72)
3. ($\frac{1}{4}$ of 16) $\times$ ($\frac{1}{8}$ of 72) (36)
4. $(7 \times 3) - 4^2$ (5)
5. $5 \times 99 = 100 \times 5 - ?$ (5)
6. $(3 \times 9) + (7 \times 9) = 9 \times ?$ (10)
7. $\frac{2}{3}$ of $72 = 72 \div 3 \times ?$ (2)
8. $(17 - 9) \times 6$ (48)
9. $36 \div 4 \times 50$ (450)
10. $(15 + 7 \times 5) \div 10$ (5)

REVIEW 7

1. 8×4 (32)
2. $13 - 8$ (5)
3. Next? 2.03 2.33 2.63 ? (2.93)
4. 120 km/h for 3 hrs (360 km)
5. 5:30 a.m. + $4\frac{1}{2}$ hrs (10 a.m.)
6. Divide 560 by 8 (70)
7. Product of 0.4×6 (2.4)
8. Next? 36 72 144 288 ? (576)
9. $7\frac{1}{2}$ hours = ? mins (450)
10. $(7 + 9) \div (13 - 9)$ (4)

Unit 36 Number Facts

1. $48 \div 4$ (12)
2. 9×8 (72)
3. 21 minus 12 (9)
4. Divide 36 by 4 (9)
5. 24 @ £5 each (£120)
6. 5×0 (0)
7. Multiply 1.2 by 4 (4.8)
8. $15 - 9$ (6)
9. 144 among 12 (12)
10. 7×6 (42)

Unit 37 Area & Perimeter

What is the perimeter of...

1. a square with sides 4 cm (16 cm)
2. a rectangle 8 cm by 10 cm? (36 cm)
3. a hexagon with sides 50 mm? (300 mm)
4. a square with sides 1.5 m? (6 m)
5. a rectangle 2.5 cm by 3 cm? (11 cm)

What is the area of ...

6. a square with sides 8 m? (64 m^2)
7. a square with sides 1.1 m? (1.21 m^2)
8. a rectangle 4 m by 9 m (36 m^2)
9. a rectangle 15 m by 5 m? (75 m^2)
10. a rectangle with sides 10 cm? (100 cm^2)

Unit 38 Fractions, Decimals, %

1. As a fraction 45% ($\frac{45}{100}$ or $\frac{9}{20}$)
2. As a decimal $\frac{4}{5}$ (0.8)
3. $\frac{5}{6}$ of 30 (25)
4. As a percentage $\frac{3}{5}$ (60%)
5. $\frac{1}{3} + \frac{1}{6}$ ($\frac{3}{8}$)
6. $\frac{5}{8}$ of 24 (15)
7. $0.8 + 0.4$ (1.2)
8. As a fraction 8.25 ($8\frac{1}{4}$)
9. 9×0.5 (4.5)
10. $\frac{3}{4} - \frac{3}{8}$ ($\frac{3}{8}$)

Unit 39 Mass, Length, Capacity

1. 700 m + 1.6 km (2.3 km)
2. 8 kg @ £4.20 a kilo (£33.60)
3. 250 ml @ £2.40 a litre (60p)
4. $\frac{3}{4}$ of 1 litre (750 ml)
5. 1.1 km − 650 m (450 m)
6. 9×1.5 l (13.5 l)
7. 15 km/h for 6 hrs = ? km (90 km)
8. ml in 1.95 l (1950 ml)
9. 4.6 kg + 575 g (5.175 kg or 5175 g)
10. metres in 5.05 km (5050)

Unit 40 Terms

1. Sum of 8 and 4 (12)
2. Product of 8 and 4 (32)
3. Quotient of 8 and 4 (2)
4. Difference between 8 and 4 (4)
5. The numerator of $\frac{5}{6}$ (5)
6. 23 minus 9 (14)
7. Perimeter of a square with sides 4.5 m (18 m)
8. Area of a rectangle 6 m by 4 m (24 m^2)
9. 7 squared (49)
10. The denominator of $\frac{3}{4}$ (4)

REVIEW 8

1. $\frac{1}{4}$ of 1 kilogram (250 g)
2. 9×6 (54)
3. As a decimal $\frac{1}{5}$ (0.2)
4. Perimeter of a rectangle 8 cm by 9 cm (34 cm)
5. 750 g @ £8.48 a kilo (£6.36)
6. mm in 3.2 metres (3200)
7. 250 ml @ £3.20 per litre (80p)
8. 750 g + 1.4 kg (2.15 kg or 2150 g)
9. As a fraction 1.25 ($1\frac{1}{4}$)
10. As a percentage $\frac{7}{20}$ (35%)

Answers

Unit 1 p. 10

A	B	C	D
1 12	1 70	1 28	1 49
2 30	2 12	2 36	2 7
3 8	3 5	3 10	3 36
4 40	4 5	4 8	4 6
5 5	5 36	5 80	5 64
6 9	6 4	6 5	6 72
7 18	7 50	7 54	7 5
8 12	8 8	8 4	8 81
9 18	9 28	9 30	9 6
10 4	10 7	10 9	10 24

Think About It! WonderGal £70

Unit 2 p. 11

A	B	C	D
1 25	1 34	1 45	1 31
2 45	2 74	2 85	2 91
3 9	3 13	3 24	3 16
4 39	4 43	4 44	4 66
5 224	5 300	5 300	5 729
6 200	6 90	6 720	6 420
7 20	7 9	7 7200	7 4200
8 4	8 3	8 8	8 4
9 100	9 200	9 80	9 8
10 200	10 510	10 680	10 730

Think About It! 20 hits per game

Unit 3 p. 12

A	B	C	D
1 190	1 235	1 15000	1 8.9
2 150	2 164	2 120	2 570
3 260	3 56.5	3 352	3 845
4 6	4 801	4 635	4 720
5 £95	5 1058	5 1.25	5 13
6 32	6 96	6 320	6 256
7 2245	7 96	7 5500	7 36
8 8	8 6500	8 112	8 3.8
9 18	9 48	9 9	9 162
10 3	10 2.2	10 36	10 49

Think About It! a 111 223 Double then add 1
b 126 254 Double then add 2 c 17 33 Double then take 1

Unit 4 p. 13

A	B	C	D
1 30	1 28	1 9.3	1 20.79
2 4.4	2 3.3	2 2.7	2 5.2
3 $\frac{1}{2}$	3 3000	3 260	3 1200
4 5	4 5	4 6	4 9.6
5 100 cm/1 m	5 4 m 76 cm	5 280	5 2 m 40 cm
6 50	6 10	6 6 km 295 m	6 3 cm 8 mm
7 200	7 10	7 1500	7 104
8 824	8 4246	8 5300	8 2.85
9 2.75	9 655	9 67	9 4800
10 8	10 480	10 20	10 18

Think About It! The winner was WonderGal.

Unit 5 p. 14

A	B	C	D
1 6734	1 60 428	1 80 088	1 654 850
2 4078	2 50 505	2 24 706	2 100 101
3 39	3 843	3 694	3 490
4 500	4 30 000	4 8000	4 80 000
5 8 units	5 6000	5 9000	5 4000
6 5	6 4 tenths	6 1	6 64
7 30	7 4 hundredths	7 5 tenths	7 9 hundredths
8 4 tenths	8 50	8 200 000	8 60 000
9 3 tenths	9 37 units	9 240	9 760
10 150	10 60	10 $\frac{35}{100}$	10 2 hundredths

Think About It! 17 895 or 51 239

REVIEW 1 p. 15

A	B	C	D
1 72	1 42	1 56	1 81
2 8	2 8	2 9	2 7
3 6	3 6	3 9	3 4
4 6	4 5	4 8	4 6
5 567	5 1390	5 6.2	5 28
6 337	6 400	6 4	6 40
7 600	7 50 000	7 2000	7 300 000
8 5500	8 240	8 580	8 1200
9 5.69 km	9 8.45 km	9 9	9 500
10 13 km	10 280 km	10 1.5	10 200

Think About It! 9 and 7

Take a Break 1 p. 16

SoupaGuy	24	8	43	45	30
	600 000	83	36		
WonderGal	36	9	32	64	45
	90	24	7.5		
Batboy	42	6	46	55	32
	80 000	59	16		
Ribbon	72	7	33	74	26
	70 000	83	80		

Unit 6 p. 17

A	B	C	D
1 42	1 32	1 54	1 72
2 45	2 63	2 70	2 48
3 5	3 9	3 3	3 6
4 49	4 25	4 64	4 100
5 5	5 9	5 7	5 8
6 8	6 3	6 8	6 9
7 32	7 70	7 32	7 54
8 48	8 36	8 42	8 56
9 3	9 7	9 12	9 11
10 5	10 4	10 3	10 7

Think About It! 9 72 10 100 Rule: × then double

Answers

Unit 7 p. 18

A	B	C	D
1 95p	1 75p	1 85p	1 51p
2 20	2 4	2 40	2 25
3 157	3 245	3 500	3 750
4 45p	4 31p	4 £1.22	4 £1.80
5 £8.85	5 £4.50	5 £14	5 50p
6 £1	6 £2	6 £90	6 £6.40
7 10	7 20	7 10	7 50
8 5p	8 31p	8 £3.45	8 £2.05
9 £5	9 £4	9 40p	9 £12.50
10 £1.80	10 £3.25	10 £5	10 £2

Think About It! 90p + 60p + 90p + 60p = £3

Unit 8 p. 19

A	B	C	D
1 5	1 6	1 $1\frac{1}{2}$	1 9
2 12	2 4	2 $\frac{2}{6}$ or $\frac{1}{3}$	2 8
3 3	3 $\frac{2}{3}$	3 5	3 $2\frac{1}{2}$
4 4	4 $\frac{1}{2}$	4 $\frac{1}{2}$	4 2
5 5	5 $\frac{3}{4}$	5 $\frac{1}{6}$	5 21
6 3	6 1	6 $\frac{1}{10}$	6 25
7 3	7 $\frac{1}{4}$	7 1	7 $2\frac{2}{8}$ or $2\frac{1}{4}$
8 4	8 $\frac{1}{4}$	8 $\frac{5}{8}$	8 $6\frac{1}{5}$
9 4	9 $\frac{1}{3}$	9 3	9 1
10 6	10 $\frac{2}{5}$	10 2	10 $1\frac{1}{3}$

Think About It! 3 pieces

Unit 9 p. 20

A	B	C	D
1 0.1	1 $\frac{1}{2}$	1 0.9	1 0.5
2 0.7	2 $\frac{1}{10}$	2 0.7	2 0.7
3 0.5	3 $\frac{4}{10}$ or $\frac{2}{5}$	3 0.25	3 0.6
4 0.3	4 $1\frac{1}{10}$	4 1.3	4 5.4
5 0.2	5 $2\frac{7}{10}$	5 0.6	5 3.5
6 0.9	6 $8\frac{1}{2}$	6 3.5	6 2.3
7 2.1	7 $5\frac{9}{10}$	7 0.75	7 3.75
8 3.5	8 $\frac{1}{4}$	8 4.1	8 1.1
9 4.7	9 $7\frac{1}{4}$	9 0.4	9 2.5
10 1.2	10 $\frac{3}{4}$	10 7.75	10 5.25

Think About It! 1st WonderGal 750 m   2nd Batboy 500 m   3rd Ribbon 400 m   4th SoupaGuy 300 m

Unit 10 p. 21

A	B	C	D
1 9	1 9	1 5	1 7
2 9	2 54	2 10	2 4, 8
3 8	3 10, 6, 48	3 8	3 9, 3
4 26	4 40, 4	4 12	4 60
5 8	5 7	5 7	5 8
6 5, 5	6 3, 8	6 4	6 24
7 70	7 30, 6, 180	7 2	7 9
8 2	8 15, 9	8 400	8 8
9 10	9 10	9 7	9 9
10 6	10 8	10 4	10 180

Think About It! 17 2 32 11 47 14 23

REVIEW 2 p. 22

A	B	C	D
1 63	1 28	1 6	1 17
2 45	2 15	2 6	2 7
3 8	3 23	3 $\frac{1}{5}$	3 400, 100
4 4	4 60p	4 0.25	4 £12
5 8	5 £3.85	5 0.4	5 £15
6 49	6 51	6 8	6 6.3
7 6	7 £5	7 $7\frac{1}{10}$	7 $\frac{1}{2}$ or $\frac{3}{6}$
8 6	8 16	8 0.2	8 £3.75
9 36	9 1250	9 12	9 $\frac{3}{4}$
10 8	10 £5.05	10 21	10 12

Think About It! $3 \times 4 + 2 - 5 = 9$ $2 \times 5 + 3 - 4 = 9$

Take a Break 2 p. 23

1 Highest score possible 192

2 Lowest score possible 48

3 132

4 Check (e.g. Round 7 (8, 8, 5) Round 8 (5, 5, 5))

5 141

6 Check (e.g. Round 1 (8, 5, 2) Round 2 (8, 8, 2))

8 WonderGal 141

Unit 11 p. 24

A	B	C	D
1 9	1 9	1 8	1 14
2 40	2 45	2 6	2 6
3 16	3 17	3 7	3 16
4 7	4 8	4 5	4 49
5 13	5 13	5 40	5 3
6 9	6 7	6 16	6 9
7 8	7 6	7 12	7 9
8 7	8 6	8 8	8 12
9 21	9 24	9 4	9 81
10 36	10 40	10 12	10 9

Think About It! $9 \times 2 = 18$ $21 \div 3 = 7$ $8 + 5 = 13$

Unit 12 p. 25

A	B	C	D
1 150	1 270	1 315	1 465
2 40	2 500	2 20	2 200
3 15	3 45	3 12	3 5
4 2	4 100	4 6	4 5
5 90	5 210	5 135	5 630
6 11:25	6 11:55 a.m.	6 5:15 a.m.	6 6:55 p.m.
7 31	7 61	7 61	7 92
8 50	8 3	8 550	8 78
9 42	9 80	9 50	9 4
10 1:40	10 10:15	10 12:30 p.m.	10 6:15 a.m.

Think About It! a 720   b 84   c 24   d 96

75

Answers

Unit 13 p. 26

A	B	C	D
1 $\frac{4}{8}$ or $\frac{1}{2}$	1 $\frac{3}{5}$	1 $\frac{5}{6}$	1 $\frac{3}{10}$
2 $\frac{1}{6}$	2 $\frac{4}{8}$ or $\frac{1}{2}$	2 $\frac{2}{5}$	2 $\frac{1}{8}$
3 12	3 4	3 4	3 3
4 3	4 6	4 8	4 7
5 0.5	5 0.3	5 3.25	5 5.5
6 $\frac{4}{10}$ or $\frac{2}{5}$	6 $\frac{1}{2}$	6 $1\frac{3}{4}$	6 $6\frac{1}{4}$
7 1.1	7 1.5	7 7.1	7 13.5
8 0.3	8 0.5	8 0.5	8 1.5
9 2.5	9 4.2	9 18	9 8.4
10 10	10 27	10 25	10 28

Think About It! $\frac{4}{6}$ $\frac{8}{12}$ $\frac{6}{9}$ $\frac{10}{15}$ $\frac{20}{30}$
Other answers are possible for the fractions circled.

Unit 14 p. 27

A	B	C	D
1 76 482	1 7894	1 185 423	1 2 636 005
2 90 468	2 50 000	2 8 hundredths	2 57 000
3 76	3 57 582	3 487 069	3 894 529
4 4	4 43 761	4 588 264	4 105 000.11
5 30 000	5 8	5 73 000	5 16 hundredths
6 8	6 $\frac{25}{100}$	6 95.37	6 6 659 278
7 694	7 73 941	7 5 860 900	7 567 259.18
8 86	8 6 tenths	8 26 hundredths	8 400
9 5 tenths	9 360	9 50	9 500 000
10 11 001	10 86.2	10 70 000	10 17 million

Think About It! China 1 188 000 000, Egypt 55 200 000, Algeria 26 346 000, Australia 18 500 000, Israel 5 000 000, Seychelles. 76 000

Unit 15 p. 28

A	B	C	D
1 420	1 60	1 960	1 163
2 108	2 112	2 1900	2 457
3 126	3 186	3 1340	3 1474
4 164	4 302	4 1514	4 1918
5 230	5 118	5 782	5 626
6 125	6 115	6 245	6 824
7 315	7 272	7 176	7 1190
8 230	8 81	8 454	8 12 146
9 36	9 74	9 620	9 169
10 290	10 668	10 903	10 48.4

Think About It! 304

REVIEW 3 p. 29

A	B	C	D
1 9	1 21	1 8	1 63
2 19	2 56	2 22	2 9
3 54	3 9	3 48	3 14
4 6	4 7	4 13	4 24
5 1:45	5 9:30	5 7:40	5 3:50
6 $\frac{1}{2}$ or $\frac{4}{8}$	6 $1\frac{3}{5}$	6 12	6 25
7 50	7 10	7 105	7 80
8 60 000	8 652.37	8 854 927	8 3500
9 1530	9 463	9 1064	9 286
10 1.3	10 0.4	10 3	10 18.4

Think About It! Check (13, 9, 20) (14, 9, 19) (15, 9, 18) (16, 9, 17)

Take a Break 3 p. 30

10	6

8	12

Unit 16 p. 31

A	B	C	D
1 30	1 63	1 28	1 12
2 9	2 9	2 42	2 36
3 40	3 2	3 4	3 6
4 56	4 11	4 3	4 16
5 8	5 32	5 3	5 64
6 8	6 9	6 7	6 2
7 36	7 0	7 3	7 9
8 6	8 8	8 8	8 49
9 0	9 54	9 2	9 56
10 8	10 49	10 27	10 108

Think About It! $4 \times 9 \div 3 = 12$

Unit 17 p. 32

A	B	C	D
1 32	1 9	1 72	1 30
2 10	2 10, 15	2 £17	2 30
3 28	3 17	3 27	3 £32
4 15	4 125, 225	4 20	4 60
5 5	5 10, 120	5 20	5 10
6 3000	6 21	6 10	6 28
7 £60	7 £15	7 12	7 50
8 4	8 72	8 3, 3, 24	8 17
9 1	9 150	9 48	9 12
10 5	10 11	10 60	10 4

Think About It! $9 \times 4 + 7 \times 4 + 6 \times 2 = 76$

Unit 18 p. 33

A	B	C	D
1 710 g	1 7.9 kg	1 4.35 kg	1 6.15 kg
2 3	2 2.6 kg	2 6.6 kg	2 5.6 kg
3 63 kg	3 16.5 kg	3 20 kg	3 8.2 kg
4 3 kg	4 400 g	4 0.8 kg	4 2.15 kg
5 5.7 kg	5 2.5 kg	5 3.2 kg	5 755 g
6 8.5 kg	6 4.6 kg	6 £1.20	6 40p
7 £6	7 £6	7 75p	7 £1.20
8 2.5	8 500	8 1500	8 10 500 kg
9 1200	9 2.25	9 1.4 kg	9 0.9 kg
10 50 g	10 5300	10 8.75 kg	10 225 g

Think About It! 1.5 kg

Answers

Unit 19 p. 34

A	B	C	D
1 50%	1 $\frac{75}{100}$ or $\frac{3}{4}$	1 50%	1 50%
2 20%	2 $\frac{10}{100}$ or $\frac{1}{10}$	2 20%	2 10%
3 10%	3 $\frac{25}{100}$ or $\frac{1}{4}$	3 60%	3 25%
4 30%	4 1	4 10%	4 5%
5 90%	5 $\frac{22}{100}$	5 80%	5 75%
6 25%	6 $\frac{56}{100}$	6 30%	6 30%
7 75%	7 $\frac{8}{100}$	7 60%	7 20%
8 15%	8 $\frac{94}{100}$	8 80%	8 4%
9 83%	9 $\frac{17}{100}$	9 48%	9 70%
10 1%	10 $\frac{33}{100}$	10 64%	10 40%

Think About It! Slammer 80%

Unit 20 p. 35

A	B	C	D
1 72	1 78	1 337	1 7945
2 42	2 60.6	2 8284	2 50.6
3 599	3 889	3 2.25	3 $1\frac{5}{8}$
4 24.7	4 3	4 $1\frac{1}{2}$	4 5868
5 1	5 47.4	5 886	5 17 625
6 302	6 2902	6 13 234	6 419.1
7 750.3	7 8532	7 1345	7 512
8 243	8 3845	8 23.1	8 6433
9 1	9 5073	9 490	9 56
10 366	10 6213	10 51.6	10 22.75

Think About It! a 2.02 20.2 20.22 2020 2202
b 0.15 0.5 1.5 15 15.5 150

REVIEW 4 p. 36

A	B	C	D
1 63	1 42	1 81	1 64
2 28	2 20%	2 $\frac{1}{2}$	2 10%
3 5 units	3 2.8	3 60p	3 4 tenths
4 £9	4 21	4 16, 80	4 150
5 210	5 12	5 2.3	5 16.1
6 158	6 £3	6 8	6 $\frac{1}{4}$
7 £7	7 128	7 6	7 £15
8 844	8 2:10 p.m.	8 570	8 7541
9 6	9 296	9 854	9 27
10 3	10 9 kg	10 9.6	10 2.5 kg

Think About It! 18 m

Take a Break 4 p. 37

Check

Unit 21 p. 38

A	B	C	D
1 35	1 32	1 54	1 56
2 6	2 3	2 2	2 9
3 4	3 11	3 8	3 9
4 5	4 6	4 5	4 8
5 13	5 17	5 11	5 15
6 6	6 8	6 6	6 5
7 0	7 8	7 64	7 24
8 10	8 7	8 0	8 5
9 49	9 0	9 35	9 0
10 36	10 25	10 9	10 81

Think About It! Check

Unit 22 p. 39

A	B	C	D
1 85	1 53	1 6	1 28 000
2 300	2 250	2 5600	2 8140
3 420	3 93	3 630	3 410
4 1520	4 647	4 170	4 7
5 80	5 18 000	5 500	5 1000
6 1000	6 420	6 760	6 60 000
7 88	7 3	7 1270	7 80
8 2900	8 689	8 70	8 750
9 10	9 3400	9 350 000	9 7600
10 8000	10 545	10 545	10 400

Think About It! 144

Unit 23 p. 40

A	B	C	D
1 900 ml	1 5.7 l	1 4.35 l	1 6.05 l
2 4 l	2 3.5 l	2 5.6 l	2 15.7 l
3 56 l	3 32.5 l	3 7.2 l	3 1.8 l
4 3.5 l	4 300 ml	4 £1.75	4 900 ml
5 8.2 l	5 525 ml	5 £4	5 30p
6 6.2 l	6 10.2 l	6 15 000	6 1.36 l
7 £1.25	7 £4.10	7 2.8 l	7 250
8 7.2 l	8 0.9 l	8 10.4 l	8 £9
9 5300	9 2.25 l	9 6.525 l	9 7.1 l
10 50 ml	10 8600	10 4.75 l	10 4.4 l

Think About It! 5 bottles and 5.5 litres left over

Unit 24 p. 41

A	B	C	D
1 180	1 4	1 48	1 10
2 4	2 5	2 7	2 60
3 40, 312	3 55	3 140	3 45
4 £55	4 10, 8	4 27	4 £32
5 16	5 54	5 4	5 60
6 62	6 8	6 20	6 3
7 9	7 60	7 10	7 247
8 12	8 5, 40	8 4	8 6, 4
9 48	9 7	9 125	9 2
10 52	10 10	10 56	10 28

Think About It! £1.30 loss

Answers

Unit 25 p. 42

A	B	C	D
1 33	1 3000	1 104	1 8.96
2 84	2 7.5	2 64	2 1.28
3 78	3 86	3 85.7	3 0.8004
4 2	4 2165	4 0.75	4 116
5 773	5 7053	5 87.91	5 $\frac{12}{16}$
6 24.6	6 70.4	6 1462	6 9000
7 $1\frac{1}{3}$	7 $2\frac{1}{4}$	7 $1\frac{2}{5}$	7 26.75
8 776	8 5318	8 3.9	8 9845
9 2662	9 528.1	9 96	9 $2\frac{1}{6}$
10 54.6	10 $\frac{7}{8}$	10 $\frac{3}{8}$	10 3969

Think About It! 101.001 101.101 110.101 111.101 101 010 110 101 111 001

REVIEW 5 p. 43

A	B	C	D
1 17	1 7	1 7	1 16
2 30	2 7	2 3	2 9
3 3	3 15	3 6	3 48
4 7	4 7	4 16	4 7
5 £3.50	5 £1.10	5 £12	5 £4.50
6 400	6 1300	6 8, 16	6 £3.90
7 8	7 70	7 3	7 1
8 35	8 4	8 2623	8 25
9 1.2 l	9 9.1 l	9 2.35 l	9 540 000
10 26	10 58	10 7500	10 170

Think About It! £300

Take a Break 5 p. 44

THE REWARD OF A THING WELL DONE

IS TO HAVE DONE IT

Unit 26 p. 45

A	B	C	D
1 8	1 13	1 7	1 10
2 35	2 24	2 94	2 6
3 52	3 24	3 36	3 64
4 5	4 46	4 16	4 54
5 49	5 4	5 8	5 154
6 19	6 7	6 24	6 118
7 8	7 4	7 10	7 42
8 9	8 34	8 8	8 9
9 4	9 36	9 58	9 12
10 0	10 12	10 9	10 7

Think About It! 1 72   2 9   3 8   4 £54

Unit 27 p. 46

A	B	C	D
1 £9.50	1 £4.55	1 £23.50	1 £2.65
2 4	2 20	2 25	2 50
3 135	3 275	3 315	3 40p
4 £7.50	4 65p	4 £6.25	4 £13.85
5 £9.55	5 £6.25	5 75p	5 £1.25
6 £7.50	6 £12.50	6 125	6 1465
7 5	7 50	7 £8.70	7 £11.50
8 £2.60	8 £1.35	8 £56	8 £6.55
9 £3	9 £4	9 £2.50	9 £2.25
10 £2.40	10 £1.75	10 £10.50	10 £12

Think About It! Ribbon £52

Unit 28 p. 47

A	B	C	D
1	1 4	1 9	1 5
2	2 3	2 4	2 2
3	3 2	3 8	3 5
4	4 2	4 2	4 3
5	5 5	5 9	5 3
6	6 8	6 5	6 7
7	7 4	7 3	7 2
8	8 10	8 5	8 6
9	9 9	9 6	9 2
10 Check	10 5	10 3	10 9

Think About It! star 4 triangle 2 square 3 circle 5

Unit 29 p. 48

A	B	C	D
1 $2\frac{1}{2}$	1 $2\frac{1}{3}$	1 $2\frac{3}{4}$	1 $3\frac{5}{6}$
2 $\frac{7}{4}$	2 $\frac{9}{4}$	2 $\frac{11}{3}$	2 $\frac{19}{4}$
3 2	3 5	3 8	3 15
4 18	4 4	4 4.7	4 4.25
5 0.7	5 0.25	5 2.1	5 2.6
6 $\frac{1}{2}$	6 $\frac{3}{4}$	6 $3\frac{7}{10}$	6 $9\frac{1}{2}$
7 1.1	7 6.8	7 0.5	7 3.1
8 0.6	8 36	8 72	8 7.2
9 4	9 75	9 30	9 75
10 25	10 $\frac{81}{100}$	10 9	10 24

Think About It! SoupaGuy 40   Batboy 92   WonderGal 80   Ribbon 80

Unit 30 p. 49

A	B	C	D
1 82 467	1 8003	1 376 539	1 50 650.75
2 7070	2 60 000	2 7700.7	2 100 000
3 24	3 256 094	3 300 000	3 37 hundredths
4 6, tenths	4 240	4 640	4 306 920
5 40	5 hundredths	5 17 units	5 6 437 269
6 4	6 35 652	6 8 373 263	6 25 000
7 832	7 50 608	7 89 568	7 4568.97
8 95	8 75	8 13 hundredths	8 4 hundredths
9 6 tenths	9 5 hundredths	9 8 hundredths	9 860.29
10 4404.4	10 87.99	9 689.32	10 1.7 million

Think About It! Brecon Beacons 135 100, Exmoor 69 280, Lake District 229 200, Snowdonia 214 160, Yorkshire Dales 176 870

78

Answers

REVIEW 6 p. 50

A	B	C	D
1 11	1 7	1 7	1 18
2 24	2 7	2 7	2 6
3 4	3 24	3 9	3 56
4 7	4 11	4 11	4 8
5 £4.20	5 £10.80	5 £18.90	5 90p
6 Check	6 2, 4	6 2, 4	6 4
7 $\frac{3}{4}$	7 3.4	7 80	7 $\frac{5}{6}$
8 50	8 £6.15	8 £8.35	8 £12
9 1.8	9 $1\frac{3}{5}$	9 $\frac{7}{10}$	9 £7
10 7596	10 86 000	10 $\frac{3}{100}$	10 76.35

Think About It! 1440

Take a Break 6 p. 51

Across
1 5600
3 144
5 24
6 108
7 1240
10 600
11 900
12 261
13 30
14 6606
16 18
18 500 000

Down
1 525
2 64
3 100 906
4 48
6 14
7 101 010
8 20
9 10
10 66
12 2995
13 36
15 695
17 80

Unit 31 p. 52

A	B	C	D
1 24	1 40	1 10	1 54
2 21	2 54	2 5	2 7
3 30	3 8	3 11	3 9
4 8	4 6	4 100	4 6
5 5	5 8	5 12	5 36
6 15	6 9	6 3	6 7
7 15	7 9	7 35	7 35
8 48	8 4	8 7	8 5
9 8	9 4	9 5	9 12
10 25	10 81	10 48	10 5

Think About It! a − 2 × 3 : 21 12 18 24 9 15
b + 6 ÷ 3 : 4 7 6 9 8 12

Unit 32 p. 53

A	B	C	D
1 4	1 10	1 32	1 52
2 100	2 8	2 29	2 55
3 25	3 12	3 130	3 4
4 16	4 100	4 72	4 300
5 64	5 7	5 11	5 44
6 36	6 2	6 84	6 4
7 81	7 0	7 36	7 2500
8 49	8 11	8 360	8 1604
9 9	9 9	9 64	9 3500
10 10 000	10 5	10 164	10 128

Think About It! 3^2 3^2 16 4^2 9 16 25 5^2 5^2 11 25 36 6^2 6^2 13 36 13 49 7^2

Unit 33 p. 54

A	B	C	D
1 195	1 450	1 345	1 735
2 half	2 540	2 36 km	2 60
3 45	3 40	3 35	3 50
4 1 15	4 30	4 10:30 a.m.	4 8 10
5 49	5 375	5 28	5 61
6 225	6 8:05	6 540	6 11:15
7 40	7 750	7 $9\frac{1}{4}$	7 615
8 4 o'clock	8 11:55	8 1:20	8 9:25
9 3 o'clock	9 30	9 6	9 14
10 10:35	10 8:15	10 7:05	10 9:30 p.m.

Think About It! 76 seconds 1 min 16 seconds

Unit 34 p. 55

A	B	C	D
1 32	1 43	1 $1\frac{7}{8}$	1 16.8
2 122	2 35.4	2 112.3	2 $1\frac{1}{2}$
3 10.7	3 495	3 1002	3 4495
4 641	4 $\frac{9}{16}$	4 4	4 £8.50
5 2621	5 9864	5 5126	5 $\frac{11}{10}$
6 1013	6 54.35	6 5.15	6 66 908
7 1	7 $1\frac{1}{2}$	7 3687	7 9800
8 512	8 576	8 8628	8 100
9 3	9 1.25	9 600.5	9 0.750
10 2684	10 42 420	10 44	10 10.007

Think About It! a 17 25 33 41 49 57 65 73 81 89 97 105
b 8.6 9.8 11 12.2 13.4 14.6 15.8 17 18.2 19.4 20.6 21.8 23
c 9462 9322 9252 9182 9112 9042 8972 8902

Unit 35 p. 56

A	B	C	D
1 300	1 12	1 6	1 55
2 8	2 25	2 72	2 10
3 6, 5	3 36	3 £16	3 88
4 £29	4 80	4 8	4 18, 16
5 72	5 6	5 36	5 0
6 6	6 27	6 4	6 240
7 7	7 54	7 47, 376	7 16, 7
8 45	8 40	8 156	8 £21
9 12	9 8	9 4	9 2^3 or 8
10 76	10 3	10 72	10 3

Think About It! 1 10 2 16 3 £320 4 Check

REVIEW 7 p. 57

A	B	C	D
1 13	1 7	1 9	1 16
2 27	2 5	2 3	2 6
3 5	3 28	3 5	3 45
4 9	4 7	4 17	4 8
5 49	5 9	5 100	5 119
6 315	6 95	6 120	6 84
7 80	7 197	7 $1\frac{1}{8}$	7 8985
8 1	8 £19	8 35	8 160
9 60 km	9 65	9 1:50	9 9 10
10 81	10 12	10 6	10 80, 1360

Think About It! 9; 28; 27 11; 17 24 7; 11 9 4; 34 15 7

79

Answers

Take a Break 7 p. 58

Quick Grid 1
16 11 13 12 8 15 14
11 6 8 7 3 10 9
17 12 14 13 9 16 15
12 7 9 8 4 11 10
9 4 6 5 1 8 7
19 14 16 15 11 18 17
18 13 15 14 10 17 16

Quick Grid 2
24 6 9 15 0 21 27
16 4 6 10 0 14 18
32 8 12 20 0 28 36
64 16 24 40 0 56 72
80 20 30 50 0 70 90
48 12 18 30 0 42 54
56 14 21 35 0 49 63

Ladder Grid
12 27
12 32
14 49
14 48
9 20
9 18
14 45
18 80
13 36
15 56

Web Grid
14 32 54 12 0 15
63 48 40 30 72 45

Unit 36 p. 59

A	B	C	D
1 4	1 6	1 6	1 7
2 4	2 48	2 32	2 17
3 9	3 13	3 42	3 8
4 4	4 17	4 14	4 9
5 14	5 6	5 4	5 16
6 8	6 7	6 6	6 9
7 25	7 9	7 56	7 7
8 4	8 4	8 8	8 9
9 3	9 40	9 7	9 9
10 7	10 9	10 8	10 56

Think About It! 72 42 9 9 7 8 2 8 7 8 7

Unit 37 p. 60

A	B	C	D
1 16 cm	1 10 m	1 32 cm²	1 100 cm²
2 36 cm	2 18 cm	2 21 cm²	2 60 cm
3 24 cm	3 22 m	3 54 m²	3 15 m
4 28 m	4 18 cm	4 28 cm²	4 240 cm²
5 44 m	5 26 m	5 6 m	5 20 cm
6 80 m	6 14 m	6 6 cm	6 9 m²
7 40 cm	7 114 m	7 2 mm	7 150 mm²
8 12 m	8 44 cm	8 9 cm	8 9 m²
9 32 m	9 108 m	9 8 m	9 2.5 m
10 20 cm	10 80 m	10 144 m²	10 5 m

Think About It! a Batboy's (420 m)
                    b WonderGal's (7500 m²)

Unit 38 p. 61

A	B	C	D
1 $1\frac{4}{5}$	1 $2\frac{5}{6}$	1 $5\frac{3}{4}$	1 $4\frac{1}{3}$
2 $\frac{7}{5}$	2 $\frac{14}{5}$	2 $\frac{16}{5}$	2 $\frac{41}{8}$
3 3	3 6	3 8	3 21
4 4.75	4 9.25	4 6.55	4 2.12
5 0.3	5 0.2	5 3.7	5 6.6
6 $\frac{7}{10}$	6 $\frac{3}{10}$	6 $\frac{3}{4}$	6 $7\frac{35}{100}$
7 4.7	7 0.3	7 3.3	7 6.25
8 20	8 5.6	8 14.4	8 97.5
9 $\frac{76}{100}$	9 70	9 75	9 60
10 15	10 $\frac{1}{5}$ or $\frac{20}{100}$	10 $\frac{18}{100}$	10 $\frac{120}{100}$

Think About It! $\frac{1}{10}$ 023 25% 30% 0.5 $\frac{3}{5}$ $\frac{3}{4}$

Unit 39 p. 62

A	B	C	D
1 2.35 kg	1 40p	1 7900	1 9.15 l
2 50 cm	2 8300	2 340 cm	2 5 9
3 3.6 l	3 1.1 l	3 120 g	3 £2
4 4.5 l	4 3.8 kg	4 5800	4 6.54 kg
5 270	5 5 94	5 £1.80	5 5.22 km
6 6.25 kg	6 £3.30	6 3600	6 £1.60
7 £1.40	7 £10.50	7 £2.10	7 7.75 l
8 £8.25	8 2.4	8 5500	8 2.4 kg
9 9.38 m	9 800 ml	9 7.55 m	9 9 m
10 3.75 kg	10 150	10 6.2 l	10 35.5

Think About It! 1 180 l   2 150 kg

Unit 40 p. 63

A	B	C	D
1 17	1 14.3	1 3.2	1 $3 \times 3 \times 3 = 3^3$
2 96	2 16	2 45.3	2 220
3 8	3 108	3 12	3 40
4 8	4 48	4 62	4 35
5 9.5	5 90	5 2550	5 1.4
6 0.8	6 £8.44	6 1.44 m²	6 300 minus 3
7 1.8	7 36 cm²	7 34 m	7 $8 \times 8 = 8^2$
8 12	8 39	8 355 ml	8 0.8 l
9 42	9 1694	9 137	9 1.3
10 0.9	10 £193	10 25	10 0.3

Think About It! Check

REVIEW 8 p. 64

A	B	C	D
1 13	1 4	1 9	1 24
2 32	2 8	2 6	2 11
3 5	3 54	3 6	3 42
4 7	4 7	4 13	4 5
5 32 cm	5 81 m²	5 20 cm 24 cm²	5 48 cm 80 cm²
6 $\frac{5}{8}$	6 8	6 $1\frac{5}{8}$	6 36
7 7.455	7 90p	7 88 5	7 7400
8 £90	8 18.2 kg	8 £3.60	8 4.225 l
9 0.2	9 $\frac{16}{10}$ or $1\frac{6}{10}$	9 25	9 57.5
10 4.2	10 7.2	10 $\frac{11}{16}$	10 5.7

Think About It! 12 and 5

Take a Break 8 p. 65

Check